Exploring Key Issues in Education

Also available from Continuum

Education Policy, Practice and Professionalism, Jane Bates and Susan Lewis

An Introduction to Education Studies, Sue Warren

An Introduction to the Study of Education, Jane Bates and Susan Lewis

Justice and Equality in Education, Lorella Terzi

Multiculturalism and Education, Richard Race

Perspectives on Participation and Inclusion, Joanna Haynes and Suanne Gibson

Theory and Practice of Education, David Turner

Exploring Key Issues in Education

Edited by

Derek Kassem and Dean Garratt

continuum

Continuum International Publishing Group

The Tower Building   80 Maiden Lane
11 York Road   Suite 704
London SE1 7NX   New York NY 10038

www.continuumbooks.com

© Derek Kassem, Dean Garratt and Contributors 2009

British Library Cataloguing-in-Publication Data
A catalogue record for this book is available from the British Library.

ISBN: 978-1-8470-6084-6 (paperback)

Library of Congress Cataloging-in-Publication Data
Exploring key issues in education / edited by Derek Kassem and Dean Garratt.
     p. cm.
   ISBN: 978-1-84706-084-6 (pbk.)
1. Education – Great Britain. 2. Education – Social aspects. I. Kassem, Derek.
II. Garratt, Dean, 1970– III. Title.
LA632.E97 2009
370.941–dc22   2008047957

Typeset by Newgen Imaging Systems Pvt Ltd, Chennai, India
Printed and bound in Great Britain by CPI Antony Rowe, Chippenham, Wiltshire

Contents

Acknowledgements

The editors would like to thank our contributors for willing to be part of this book and to Jo Allcock for her support and encouragement with the project. We would also like to thank our families for their ongoing support without which projects such as this book would not be possible: Jackie, Clara, Claire, Tom and the newest member William.

Contributors

Professor Mark Brundrett is professor of Educational Research and Head of the Centre for Research and Evaluation at Liverpool John Moores University

Marilyn Eccles is the leader of the Centre for Urban Education and the director of Urban Education in Manchester, Manchester Metropolitan University

Dr Dean Garratt is a senior lecturer in Education Studies at Liverpool John Moores University

Professor David Hursh is associate professor of teaching and curriculum in the Warner Graduate School of Education at the University of Rochester

Dr Russell Jones is a senior lecturer in Early Childhood Studies at Manchester Metropolitan University

Derek Kassem is a principal lecturer in Education Studies and Deputy Centre Leader of the Centre for Education Studies and Primary Education, Liverpool John Moores University

Dr Kate MacDonald was formerly a senior lecturer and course leader Education Studies at the University of Worcester

Elaine Mitchell is a lecturer in Childhood Studies at Manchester Metropolitan University

Emmanuel Mufti was formerly a senior lecturer in Education Studies at Liverpool John Moores University

Lisa Murphy is a principal lecturer in Education Studies and deputy centre leader of the Centre for Education Studies and Primary Education, Liverpool John Moores University

Dr Heather Piper is a senior research fellow in the Education and Social Research Institute, Manchester Metropolitan University

John Robinson was director of research in the Centre for Urban Education, Manchester Metropolitan University

Dr Gabriella Torstensson is a senior lecturer in Early Childhood Studies, Liverpool John Moores University

Dr Terry Wrigley is a senior lecturer in Education, University of Edinburgh

Abbreviations

ABCD	Assets-Based Community Development
AIDS	Acquired Immune Deficiency Syndrome
ARK	Absolute Return for Kids
ART	Antiretroviral Treatment
AYP	Adequate Yearly Progress
BAEO	Black Alliance for Educational Options
BBC	British Broadcasting Corporation
BIDPA	Botswana Institute for Development Policy Analysis
BME	Black and Minority Ethnicity
BSF	Building Schools for the Future
CfBT	Centre for British Teachers Education Trust
CTC	City Technology College
DCSF	Department for Children, Schools and Families
DES	Department of Education and Science
DfEE	Department for Education and Employment
DfES	Department of Education and Skills
ECM	Every Child Matters
ERA	Education Reform Act
EU	European Union
FSM	Free School Meals
GCSE	General Certificate of Secondary Education
GNVQ	General National Vocational Qualification
HIV	Human Immunodeficiency Virus
HMI	Her Majesty's Inspectorate
HMIE	Her Majesty's Inspectorate in Education
ICT	Information Communication Technology
IQ	Intelligence Quotient
LA	Local Authority
LEA	Local Education Authority
LMS	Local Management of Schools
MEP	Member of the European Parliament
NAA	National Assessment Agency
NACA	National AIDS Coordinating Agency
NAEP	National Assessment of Educational Progress

NC	National Curriculum
NCB	National Children's Bureau
NCLB	No Child Left Behind Act
NEET	(Young People) Not in Employment, Education or Training
NFER	National Foundation for Educational Research
NGO	Non-Governmental Organisation
NHS	National Health Service
NUT	National Union of Teachers
NVQ	National Vocational Qualification
NYSSBA	New York State Schools Boards Association
OECD	Organisation for Economic Cooperation and Development
Ofsted	Office for Standards in Education
PFI	Private Finance Initiative
PISA	Program in International Student Assessment
PLASC	Pupil Level Annual School Census
PPP	Public Private Partnership
QCA	Qualifications and Curriculum Authority
RISE	Research and Information on State Education
SATs	Standard Assessment Tasks
SEN	Special Educational Need
SER	School Effectiveness Research
SEU	Social Exclusion Unit
TGAT	Task Group on Assessment Testing
UDHR	Universal Declaration of Human Rights
UNAIDS	Joint United Nations Programme on HIV/AIDS
UNCRC	United Nations Convention on the Rights of the Child
UNICEF	United Nations Children's Fund
VCG	Vulnerable Children's Grant

Introduction

This book sets out to examine some of the key issues that face education today, both at home within the UK and globally abroad. While the book does not claim to be fully comprehensive, or even provide a definitive analysis of key current issues, it does focus on a significant range of educational themes, challenges and twenty-first-century dilemmas. The intention throughout is to provide a series of chapters that critically challenge the reader to question aspects of dominant thinking, current orthodoxy, policy and practice. That is, dominant thinking in relation to, first, the influence of so-called political modernizations: school systems, assessment procedures and educational freedom. These chapters question the value of current policy initiatives that are impacting upon and serving to restructure the education system, and which have the pernicious effect of perpetuating winners and losers, generating forms of disaffection and exclusion along the way. The first of these, in Part One, by Kassem and Garratt, takes an overview of the last 20 years to examine the continuous and unrelenting neo-liberal drift of educational policy, in terms of identifying and charting right-wing ideological movements within UK education. By focusing upon the social, political and economic factors in education, a substantive context is set for the discussion and analysis of key issues that follow. In this vein, Wrigley surgically cuts through the government's rhetoric of diversity and opportunity, ostensibly embedded within the Academies programme, to expose its purpose: the privatization of secondary education. Continuing with the theme of privatization and open competition, MacDonald conducts a critical analysis of the current assessment and testing regime. Under the guise of meritocracy, she argues that the influence of external forms of assessment, operating within a culture of performativity and accountability, create the illusion rather than the possibility of self-improvement, through an outcome-based approach that focuses on the needs of those who control the system, at the expense of teacher assessment and pupil learning. The chapter by Jones and Mitchell further explores the process of unpicking key elements in government rhetoric: freedom, autonomy and choice, which they identify as an educational 'myth' or rhetorical gloss which paints over the real workings of the educational market. In reality, this is a quasi-market in which the individual is constrained by their social environment, with limited real choices aligned to the politics of knowledge, power and control.

Following Part One, the book addresses the theme of marginalization and education. Building upon the critical orientation of the early chapters, this part of the book draws attention to exemplar themes of the losers and beneficiaries and losers identified within systems, procedures and notions of freedom. It does so by explicitly focusing upon a series of recursive and enduring issues that lay at the heart of the theme of marginalization of excluded communities. The first of these chapters, by Kassem and Murphy, examines how institutional mechanisms based on faith operate to include already privileged groups within society. As part of the New Labour agenda, faith schools represent the latest move in the bid to continue to privilege large sections of education and formal schooling. In the next chapter, Mufti discusses the continuation of the systematic failure and exclusion of white working-class kids. The analysis of this issue explores how various institutional procedures and structures in education continue to disadvantage children from less-privileged backgrounds, presenting them as victims of their own intellectual and cultural inadequacies, in ways that ritually exclude them from receiving opportunities to achieve academic success. On a similar theme, Garratt and Piper examine the plight of gypsies and travellers and argue that despite many interventions by successive governments, both within and outside education, to improve their experience little obvious progress has been made. Much in the way that white working-class kids are often socially disadvantaged by forms of negative stereotyping, gypsy and traveller children are typically caricatured in a manner that serves to 'fix' their identity, adding to their problems within education and sealing their marginalization from schools. Continuing with and further developing the critique of structural inequalities, Robinson and Eccles focus on the theme of education in the inner city. They explore urban education and focus on what they refer to as the 'hyperconcentration' and density of disadvantage that faces educators and learners alike.

The third part reflects upon the structural barriers and policy impediments that inhibit the development of holistic approaches to teaching and learning: approaches that should meet the needs of all young people. It extends its critical focus beyond UK boundaries to explore a range of apparently intractable global dilemmas and consider their attendant implications for inclusive education in Europe, Africa and the US. The first, by Kassem, compares and contrasts the provision made for looked-after children in the UK and Europe. It questions the effectiveness of the Every Child Matters (ECM) agenda and problematizes the inherent lack of holistic support for looked-after children in the UK compared with the rest of Europe. It is argued that the chronic failure to address the needs of looked-after children in the UK is a consequence of the historical antecedents of social policy and performative culture within the field of social care. In their chapter, Torstensson and Brundrett question the dominance of the 'audit-culture' and recurring emphasis on school effectiveness research within the academic curriculum, in the context of the HIV/AIDS pandemic in Botswana. As a radical alternative, they suggest the need for a type of critical pedagogy that seeks to empower teachers and students, and combine the social and educational needs of young people, as a means to produce a holistic approach to HIV/AIDS and education. This would go some way to redefining what counts as quality within education, challenging the narrow confines of an academic curriculum. In the last chapter, Hursh critically analyses the largest single education initiative in the history of the US. Under the guise of raising academic achievement and meeting the needs of marginalized communities, the No Child Left Behind (NCLB) initiative can be seen to produce a chimera or false-notion of improvement in education behind a façade of testing, accountability and educational underfunding.

Part One
Reform: Changes for the Better?

Why do politicians always sound the same?

Derek Kassem and Dean Garratt

1

Chapter Outline

Introduction

Since the mid-1970s, educational reform has been high on the agenda of all the major political parties. To appreciate the nature and purpose of some of these changes over time it is necessary to recognize and understand the ideological forces underlying the formation of policy, during this period. The identification and exposure of the ideological atmosphere in which politicians are currently debating will allow the reader to reflect critically on a range of views expressed in this volume, across what might be viewed as a relatively diverse range of topics. Recognizing the constraints on the political nature of the educational debate will go some way to inform the commonality of concerns that run throughout each of the chapters in the book. The discussion rests upon a wide range of social and educational issues and takes place against the backdrop of a dominant discourse and political culture, through a questioning of the hegemony of current policy in the UK. This chapter, therefore, takes an overview of the last 20 years by examining the continuous and unrelenting neo-liberal drift of educational policy, identifying and charting the influence of right-wing ideological movements within the UK system. Further, by focusing upon the coalition of social, political and economic factors in education, a substantive context is set for later discussion and further critical analysis of key contemporary issues in education.

Historically, education has always been a controversial area of social policy within the UK. While there have been periods when education was a less prominent item on the agenda of the major political parties, never has there been a time in which it was not highly political, or indeed the subject of considerable and sustained rigorous debate. With this in mind, the chapter starts by reviewing the period of education policy prior to the start of the 1980s. This is to provide a context in order to make sense of the fundamental shift in social and educational policy that took place during the reign of the Conservative Government from 1979–97, and thereafter the administration of New Labour from 1997 until present.

The year of 1979 is significant for the fact that it represents not only a step-change in the direction of social and educational policy, but also perhaps a more profound and enduring ideological shift away from the previously dominant orthodoxy of the period between 1945 and 1979. The consequence of such a 'right-wing' shift, in policy discourse terms, is one which continues to be played out in current educational debates. Before discussing these issues, however, it is important to establish the historical antecedents and context leading up to 1979.

Let us Face the Future

Let us Face the Future was the title of the Labour Party manifesto for the 1945 General Election. In many ways it captured the prevailing mood of the moment and further represented the dominant ideas of the time. Following the economic recession of the 1930s and impact of the Second World War, the UK was faced not only with difficulties of having to rebuild its economic infrastructure but also with the thorny issue of how to make society a fairer place to live. Part of this process involved what was then referred to as 'a new era of social consciousness' (Kynaston, 2007: 27–8), which was subsequently reflected in the educational reforms of the 1940s, referred to as 'the greatest and grandest educational advance since 1870'. The government of the day identified its underlying philosophy as one that was embedded within the educational principles of 'equality of opportunity, and diversity of provision without impairment of the social unity' (28). The post-1945 reforms were thus socially and educationally fundamental, since, for the very first time, at least some form of secondary education would be provided for the benefit of all children. However, it is the context in which these radical reforms took place that is especially important.

The coalition government of 1944 included members of both major political parties: Conservative and Labour, along with members of the Liberal and Liberal National Parties. However, it was the Conservative Minister, Rab Butler, who managed the passing of the

Education Act through parliament, comprising a set of reforms described as part of the postwar settlement (Jones, 2003). Importantly, while there were clearly marked political differences between the parties that formed the coalition, there was general agreement on the direction of most aspects of social and educational policy. This broad consensus, exhibited through the leadership of each of the political parties on matters of social policy, nevertheless contrasted with the vagaries of the economic forces that prevailed outside the 'charmed-circle' of parliament. As Jones (ibid.: 13) points out:

> in education, the reforms of 1943–7 had been supported – outside government circles – in terms that were explicitly egalitarian as well as modernizing. They thus posed a challenge to institutions, administrative systems and ideologies which had been created by old elites, in the interests of the dominant classes. But in practice these radical impulses did not prevail.

Activity

The 1944 Education Act created a tripartite system for secondary education with the introduction of Grammar, Technical and Secondary Modern Schools. Research these different types of school and answer the following questions:

1. Do you think the tripartite system was based on an egalitarian approach to education or a system of hierarchies?
2. Who do you think were the main beneficiaries of the tripartite system of secondary education introduced in the 1940s?
3. Why do you think a government committed to social justice introduced the educational reforms that were implemented by the 1944 Act?

The constraints upon the level of educational evolution and revolution during the period are perhaps best illustrated through the Party's reluctance to accept the sustained influence and role of the private sector in education. This was something which stood in complete opposition to the more radical elements of the labour movement of the day (Simon, 1991), where the ruling ideology might well be regarded as social democratic. Of course, this is not to say that the major political parties adopted the same overtly ideological stance. Rather, it is more a case of arguing that the major social reforms of the day: education for all, the National Health Service (NHS) and other such similar forms of change, were neither dismantled by subsequent Conservative administrations, nor in fact altered to the degree that they have been since 1979. In general terms, the very language (discourse) used to describe the policies of the time was not so dissimilar. Notions of equality of opportunity, fairness and justice and economic and social progress are just some of the terms used to describe the various educational initiatives of the period. This, we argue, represents the hegemony of social democracy as the dominant ideology of social and educational policy.

Social democracy

Over time, the meaning of the term social democracy has changed in ways that have come to represent a particular political perspective. This is one that contains a firm belief in the delicate balancing act between the influence of the market economy, on the one hand, and deliberative role of the state on the other (Heywood, 2003). Social democracy is thus broadly committed to liberal democratic principles coupled with constitutional change. The pervasive influence of the market economy within capitalist society, viewed as the most efficient means of creating wealth, is considered to be fundamentally flawed in relation to the social aims of achieving equality, fairness and the elimination of poverty. In a climate of social democracy, it is acknowledged that the state needs to intervene in defence of those members of society who typically lose out in the process of wealth creation. This is done through various types of reform, a progressive system of taxation and what is commonly referred to as social engineering. Such mechanisms of state intervention can be called upon in the spirit of social unity and the national interest. Thus, for the social democrat, the nation-state represents the major political means within which key social reforms and control take place (adapted from Heywood, 2003).

In terms of education policy, from the 1940s onwards until 1979 a social democratic perspective held sway across all areas of social provision. Knight (1990) demonstrates the cultural and political dominance of social democratic thinking in his analysis of Conservative Party education policy during its 13 years of uninterrupted rule, from 1951 until 1964, pointing out that:

> It should be remembered that, during the thirteen years of Conservative government (1951–64), the number of comprehensive schools rose from five to 195; and that long before Circular 10/65,[1] sixty-eight LEAs had begun to implement concrete proposals for reorganizing secondary education, and twenty-one more were contemplating proposals. Only fifty-nine were not even considering them – probably because it was not necessary to do so in their territories. (Knight, 1990: 14)

He goes on to state that:

> Conservative Party policy on education was now largely non-partisan, promising to give primary education a high priority and, in the reorganization of secondary education, accepting the movement away from selection. (Knight, 1990: 31)

The period that Knight is commenting upon can be regarded as the height of progressive education during the 1960s. Yet it would be crude and overly simplistic to assume there was clear consensus on all matters of social and educational policy, for this was not the case. There were some serious divisions on education policy within the Conservative Party at all levels of government, both nationally and locally, and indeed some of these differences would later surface during the 1970s. However, it should also be recognized that there were some key tensions in policy within the ranks of the Labour Party too. The most obvious of which arose in relation to the acceptance by the 1945 Labour Government of a tripartite system of education based on the principle of selection: Grammar, Technical and Secondary Modern schools, and further preservation of the private sector. Commenting on the then Prime Minister, Clem Attlee's desire to avoid any radical challenge of the vested interests of the educational elite, Jones (2003) suggests that what was lacking was not so much the opportunity to debate *per se*, but rather the occasion to expose to critical scrutiny the unstated assumptions underlying the governance of society, as well as the social and moral purpose of its future direction.

The political tone and ideological atmosphere of the period can best be understood through a consideration of the reforms that took place from 1945 onwards. This period saw a major expansion in the financial support of higher education, especially in terms of the growth of teacher education and implementation of the student grant system. For the first time, this allowed working-class children to achieve comparatively smooth and easy access through to higher education. Similarly, for those at school there were generous uniform grants, free school meals (FSM) (much easier to obtain than today) and free milk for all school-aged children. These were just a few of the policies intended to address the educational needs of the ordinary child and social poverty gap.

By the 1950s, some leaders of the Labour Party, then in opposition, began to assume that the worst excesses of capitalism had been effectively reduced (Lawton, 2005). For example, one Labour leader of the day, Anthony Crosland, passionately argued that the socialist alternative must be continually restated. Indeed, just as the Conservative Party had 'moved' ideologically in terms of the social and educational policies they implemented on gaining power after 1951, so too did the political thinking of the Labour Party. So while differences persisted and debates still raged, the aims, direction and discourse of Party policies were not, at heart, fundamentally different; it was more a matter of emphasis, subtlety and nuance.

The preceding commentary presents a fairly rudimentary explanation of the way in which various forms of state intervention, through a positive concern for social justice, were employed to ease the impact of poverty on families and children leading up to 1979. These dominant concerns are most clearly recognized in the area of housing, where it was the intention of all governments pre-1979 to advertise the number of houses they had built – namely, council houses – especially in areas of marked social and economic deprivation. Indeed, as a useful way of comparing policy of the past with that of the present, the reader might usefully reflect on this fact in light of the housing policies of today (e.g. the expectation that most people will become home-owners).

Conservative debate

In spite of some areas of mutual agreement, there were, of course, a number of dissenters among the ranks of the Conservative Party, some of whom persistently argued against the reforms that were being implemented. In policy terms, one notable example was the bold move towards child-centred education and more general support, within the Party, for the liberal ideology of progressivism. At the same time, however, the right wing of the Conservative Party argued for a change back to what they considered to be more traditional standards and methods of teaching (Knight, 1990). Along with other colleagues, Rhodes Boyson, a leading Conservative educationalist and headmaster of a North London Comprehensive school, published what became collectively known as the Black Papers (Cox and Dyson, 1971). These sought to challenge the dominance of the then current orthodoxy of liberal progressivism and thus effectively attempt to realign education policy within the Conservative Party during the 1970s. While the controversial nature of ideas contained within the Black Papers were not immediately accepted by the Conservative premiership of the Heath Government, upon Thatcher's ascendancy to leadership they were quickly integrated into mainstream education policy and practice. This was especially true as the Conservative Party began to move ideologically further to the right under Thatcher and the persuasive influence of Keith Joseph (a Minster of Education under Thatcher).

Changing perspective

Towards the end of the 1970s the Conservative Party began to break with the consensus of the postwar settlement underpinned by a social-democratic (Keynesian) approach to the economy. The reasons for this change can in part be identified with the growing influence of economists such as Fredrick Hayek and Milton Friedman, both of whom argued for a market-driven economy. The persuasive influence of a *laissez-faire* approach to economic management had a profound impact on the aspirations of the neo-liberals and political right of the Conservative Party. For along with the definitive change in economic thinking came a similarly radical transformation in the nature of social and educational policy. In this, there was a fundamental shift from the notion of the state, as principal provider of economic welfare and security, towards a position in which *the invisible hand* of the market would effectively regulate all social and economic relations. As Hayek (2001: 104) states:

> economic freedom which is the perquisite of any other freedom cannot be the freedom from economic care which the socialists promise us and which can be obtained only by relieving the individual at the same time of the necessity and the power of choice; it must be the freedom of our economic activity which, with the right choice, inevitably also carries the risk and the responsibility of that right.

Thus, Hayek deems economic security to be fundamentally incompatible with social and economic freedom. This represents a radical departure from the focus of the previous governments, under the influence of the social democratic model of society: a model which sought to privilege economic and social security through state intervention. In contrast, for Hayek the supreme model of society is one that is based on the philosophy of personal responsibility and individualism, with little or no intervention by the state, which is replaced by the authority of the market. The state's role is thus consigned to ensuring that the market can operate efficiently, adopting supply-side measures (i.e. creating optimum conditions) to ensure the adequate flexibility of labour (Olssen et al., 2004), and further provide adequate law and order. The most radical and extreme example of this type of socio-economic policy in practice was implemented in Chile, under the condition of a dictatorship, following the military takeover of 1973.

Following the Conservative election victory of 1979, the dominant approach to social and economic policy was defined by a firm commitment to individualism with a reduced role for the state as a purveyor of social welfare, especially in terms of the regulation and control of economic assets. This shift in emphasis stimulated a comprehensive policy of privatization, in which the private sector became largely responsible for providing the services that had been previously regulated and supplied by the 'nanny-state' (i.e. controlled and regulated by the state). The commitment towards the market and support for the rational deliberation of consumer choice together provided a mechanism for the distribution of scarce resources. In this new paradigm of market virtue, social welfare was no longer the principal driver of social and economic policy as it had been under the influence of the social democratic model. In terms of public services such as education, the market brought an increased notion of accountability through the use of targets and measurement of performance, both of individuals and institutions. Theoretically at least, the use of competition also promised a reduction in the cost of public services, where the marketization of such services would be linked to a revised notion of the individual using them. Such individuals would no longer be regarded as students, pupils or patients but rather conceived as consumers, customers and/or clients. This stress on the consumer as opposed to the producer of public services, allows a creeping distrust of professional judgement to develop as the consumer confidently asserts their 'new-found' rights (adapted from Hill and Cole, 2004).

Changing direction

Fundamental change in the nature of social and economic policy does not happen all at once. It is often a slow and gradual process, as obstacles to power and authority and vested interests need to be vigorously challenged. This was recognized by the Attlee Government of 1945, and was initially, equally well recognized by the Thatcher administration of 1979. In the latter case, the dismantling of structures and removal of all obstacles to power first began by reducing the scope, resource and influence of Local Education Authorities (LEAs). The initial changes included removing responsibility for the polytechnics from the authority and control of LEAs, along with the abolition of the curriculum organization – the Schools Council. Interestingly, much later, this policy was further developed by New Labour under the adapted guise of City Technology Colleges (CTC). For all intents and purposes, these institutions were ostensibly schools operating outside the control of LEAs and sponsored by private business. However, CTCs were not the only schools to operate outside the control of LEAs. Previous Conservative Governments also consented to ordinary schools opting out of LEA governance, thus removing one of the key functions of local government and at the same time affirming the importance of local choice. However, the sweeping and fundamental educational reforms that served to configure the school system as we know it today did not begin until the late 1980s. The parallel reforming and restructuring of a service as large and complex as education is extremely challenging, which is, in part, due to the onerous and unpredictable nature of policy itself. Policies can be misunderstood, obstructed, reinterpreted or simply seen as unworkable given the context in which they are implemented (Ball, 2008).

The overarching aim and focus of the Conservatives was to set up the mechanisms that would create market like structures within the realm of public services. If not always explicitly stated, there was certainly a feeling within the ranks that if a service could be provided by private industry then this would automatically be the preferred or default option. Indeed, it was during this period that strongholds of municipal social democracy were effectively challenged, for services that were once carried out by local councils were now put out to private tender. For example, council housing was sold-off and a quasi-market mechanism was introduced and swiftly set up within the school system. The thrust of this policy was to embed competition within the education system. In higher education, universities are in continuous competition with each other for students, otherwise colloquially referred to as 'bums on seats', since numbers translate into income. Within the current framework, schools, just as universities, are in direct competition with each other for pupils.

Local Management of Schools (LMS)

Up until the introduction of LMS in 1988, which came about as part of a broader set of reforms under the Education Reform Act, LEAs were tasked with managing the budgets of schools under their jurisdiction and control. However, this policy initiative did two significant things: first, it took away the economic power of the LEA, thus challenging its ability to use its financial clout to control what took place in schools; second, it gave considerable power to headteachers and their management committees. The financial entitlement and allocation of resources to any one school received was based on the simple metric of the number of pupils on roll; therefore, the more pupils a school could gain the more income it would receive. Effectively, this set in motion the concept of open competition, waging school against school. In the context of the new quasi-market, parents were now recognized as consumers in need of encouragement to shop for the best school for their child/children. In time, good schools would grow, while their so-called poor neighbours would inevitably falter, falling into decline with dwindling numbers and later becoming economically unviable before finally closing. The rise to prominence of the new quasi-market would thus serve as the arbiter of quality within education through the mechanism of open competition.

Key Questions

1. What are the main characteristics of a market and are they appropriate for an education system that is supposed to serve the whole community?
2. Who do you think would be the main losers in an education market today and why?
3. Who do you think would be the main winners in an education market today and why?
4. Do you think education markets can improve the quality of education, if not, why not?

Parental choice

For LMS to work reliably and dependably, the system of how pupils were allocated to schools had to be changed. No longer would LEAs be able to offer parents merely one or two alternative schools to choose from for the education of their children. Rather, the new system had to become an authentic market (Tooley, 1997), based on genuine parental choice. This was known as open enrolment: in other words, a parent could opt for any school for their child's education. While the rhetoric sounded plausible enough, the reality was starkly different. From the very beginning there were problems of logistics and scale, both of the physical capacity of schools to accept pupils and of exorbitant travelling costs, impacting on the true extent to which parents had authentic choice of schools. Furthermore, what of the issue of informed choice? In the absence of perfect knowledge (a condition of open and authentic markets), how would parents know which is the better school in their locality? In any case, how would this be measured and where would the emphasis fall? The solution to these seemingly intractable problems was to action further reforms to the education system, all contained in the Education Reform Act (ERA) in 1988, such as the introduction of a National Curriculum, and ironically a centrally controlled assessment structure for all schools.

National Curriculum

To ensure that schools could be compared with one another the Government introduced the National Curriculum (NC). This was controversial both within the Conservative Party itself and with those carrying different political views and opinions. Resistance within the Conservative Party came from the New Right and those who wished to completely privatize the school system, believing that all schools should mimic, if not become small businesses and that survival would be based on their intrinsic ability to attract pupils. However, even the more extreme free marketers eventually came to accept the NC, which placed central government firmly and irrevocably in control. The NC represents a traditional view of what children should learn (White, 1988) and is thus highly structured with sets of attainment targets that children are expected to achieve. Through a prescriptive system of testing, the government was able to ensure that all schools were effectively producing the same supervised product, allowing for the easy comparison of performance between schools. However, it is important to note that this state of affairs did not apply to all schools equally across all parts of Britain. Private schools, operating within the 'independent sector', were exempted from following the diktat and prescription of the NC. As such, the NC fell short of being genuinely *national*; it was really no more than an English and Welsh state school curriculum. In addition, it is worth noting that teachers were generally opposed to the introduction of the NC, not least because it challenged their professional autonomy and control of the curriculum. Professional judgement was now under the watchful eye and control of the state, and so, quite obviously, this reform was situated in sharp contrast to the ideas underlying LMS; that is, ideas that were originally intended to free schools from the control of LEAs. It can therefore be argued that during the early 1990s educational policy was in fact working in diametrically opposed ways. At the same time as decentralizing the school funding system, the Government was effectively nationalizing the curriculum to be taught in all state schools in England and Wales.

Quality assurance

Through the lens of Government policy, parents, acting as consumers, in the education market place need to be sure that the goods and services that are being purchased are of sound and reputable quality. In this quasi-market the government wanted to secure and implement supervisory mechanisms that would ensure such quality. To this end, three different interlocking instruments, or tools, were introduced to the education system. The first was Standard Assessment Tasks (SATs), which all pupils in England are expected to undertake at the end of each Key Stage. However, in outcome these tests had the effect of monitoring and auditing teachers and schools as opposed to demonstrating pupil progress, the primary justification for SATs. The second instrument, school league tables, are generated through the publication of SATs results. In these, schools are pitted against each other, where the consequences of achieving poor results can impact negatively on levels of recruitment and therefore lead to a fall in income, along with a subsequent reduction in teachers' jobs. The third and final instrument is contained in the process of inspection, initiated to ensure consistency and quality across all educational processes. The language that is often employed by politicians to describe such collective processes is present in the register of choice, freedom and empowerment for the putative consumer. Since the current education system is the product of a state orchestrated market, it is also one that appropriates the language of the market as a means to describe its features. Gone is the language of equal opportunities.

New Labour

When New Labour entered government in 1997, Tony Blair declared 'No one ever believes that anything happens in education and we will prove them wrong' (cited in Seldon, 2007: 107). In making this statement, it was clear that Blair had an agenda for education and the public sector more generally, and this ideological approach eventually came to be recognized as the 'Third Way'. Theoretically at least, this perspective represented both a rejection of the old notions of social democracy (i.e. Old Labour), and the previous Conservative Government's commitment to neo-liberal economic policies and the free market (Giddens, 1998). The characteristics of the Third Way have been identified by Giddens (ibid.: 70), as follows:

- The radical centre
- The new democratic state (the state without enemies)
- Active civil society
- The democratic family
- The new mixed economy
- Equality as inclusion
- Positive welfare
- The social investment state
- The cosmopolitan nation
- Cosmopolitan democracy.

The Third Way Programme, as Giddens (ibid.) calls it, represents both a radical response by the New Labour leadership to the perceived failure of old social democratic ideals (which, it should be noted, was not insignificant in their 18-year absence from power), and reaction to the influence of a newly globalized world. In its scope and wisdom, the Third Way was supposed to transcend both the politics of the left and the right; it was to represent a new state of affairs, the politics of a newly revitalized and radical centre. In part, it was also a response to what some have referred to as the 'death of socialism', in the wake of the widespread collapse of Stalinist dictatorships across Eastern Europe. However, it should be noted that the Third Way is not uniquely British, for it was also linked to the New Democrats of the Clinton administration in the US. Irrespective of political context, then, the intellectual momentum for the Third Way is contained in its intimate relationship to the economy: 'the determining context of economic policy is the new global market' (Blair cited in Callinicos, 2001: 16). It is in this sense that the global market both impacts and drives social policy, where in the US, for example, positive welfare is translated as 'work fair'; that is, a programme in which there are no state benefits but where assistance into work is provided, usually in the form of low-paid jobs for the unemployed.

Useful Websites

The following websites are a good source of critiques of current government initiatives:

RISE – Research and Information on State Education   www.risetrust.org.uk/index.html
Socialist Education Association   www.socialisteducation.org.uk/
SATs Must Go   http://satsmustgo.tripod.com/
Education for Tomorrow   http://eddie.idx.com.au/
Anti-Academies Alliance   www.antiacademies.org.uk/

In the UK, the Third Way approach to education has seen the increased privatization of public sector services (Ball, 2007), the development of the social investment state and breakup of the school system, through the creation of new school structures that lie outside the democratic control of local government and communities:

> The seed was planted when Adonis (*a Government Minister*) visited three City Technology Colleges (CTCs) in Croydon, Telford and Gateshead. He realised that he was not just looking at individually exceptional schools: here was a model of the future schooling which had four ingredients that were to become the distinctive features of academies: independence from local authority management, successful external sponsors offering inspiring vision, a no-nonsense approach setting high standards, and finally investment in modern buildings. (Seldon, 2007: 109)

The City Academies were launched in 2001 (for a fuller discussion see Terry Wrigley's chapter in this volume), and these were quickly followed by the Specialist schools programme. However, it can be argued that whatever title or type of new programme or initiative, there is an inherent bias within current educational policy towards the 'New Right'. This effectively challenges the philosophical premise of old social democratic structures and builds on the neo-liberal influence of the previous Conservative administration. In this respect, New Labour politicians can be seen to use all but the very same language as Conservatives, so while the spin may be ever so slightly different and debates heated, in the end it is all about the margins of provision. In the current climate, it can therefore be argued that New Labour has positively accepted the hegemony of neo-liberal economic thinking that continues to dominate the (Western) industrial world. However, Britain is not unique. An examination of education policy (and its nomenclature) in almost any country in the West, will reveal similar phrases, political slogans and social and educational practices. Thus, it is argued that the operating paradigm comprises the following rationality and ideological world-view:

> Neoliberalism is in the first instance a theory of political economic practices that proposes that human well-being can best be advanced by liberating individual entrepreneurial freedoms and skills within an institutional framework characterized by strong private property rights, free markets and

free trade. The role of the state is to create and preserve an institutional framework appropriate to such practices. The state has to guarantee, for example, the quality and integrity of money. It must also set up those military, defence, police, and legal structures and functions required to secure private property rights and to guarantee, by force if need be, the proper functioning of markets. Furthermore, if markets do not exist (in areas such as land, water, education, health care, social security, or environmental pollution) then they must be created, by state action if necessary. But beyond these tasks the state should not venture. (Harvey, 2005: 2)

These are the social, political and economic ideas that currently inform social and educational policy and practice globally. Their pervasive influence also explains why so many politicians inevitably always sound the same. The intention of this volume is to present a rigorous analysis and critique of the 'sameness' of the dominant paradigm, across a broad range of educational contexts.

Key Points

- Education policy has become an increasingly central political issue over the last 30 years
- Education policy debate takes place in the context of wider social policy discourse
- Education policy from 1945 to 1979 tended to follow a social democratic/one-nation Conservative perspective
- Key elements of pre-1979 policy included a commitment to equality, social justice and equal opportunities
- A fundamental shift took place in education and social policy discourse from 1979
- Education and social policy since 1979 has been centred around notions of choice, accountability and the development of market mechanisms as the main source of resource distribution
- Education policy today exists in the context of neo-liberal free market economic and social policy.

Further Reading

Stephen Ball (2008) *The Education Debate*, Bristol: Policy Press.
Clyde Chitty (2004) *Education Policy in Britain*, London: Palgrave Macmillan.
Ken Jones (2003) *Education in Britain 1944 to the Present*, London: Polity.
Raymond Plant, Matt Beech and Kevin Hickson (2004) *The Struggle for Labour's Soul: Understanding Labour's Political Thought since 1945*, London: Routledge.

Note

1. Circular 10/65 was the Labour Government's order to Local Authorities to draw up plans for the introducing comprehensive schools.

References

Ball, S. (2008) *The Education Debate*, Bristol: Policy Press.

Ball, S. (2007) *Education PLC: Understanding Private Sector Participation in Public Sector Education*, London: Routledge.

Callinicos, A. (2001) *Against the Third Way*, London: Polity.

Cox, C. and Dyson, A. (1971) *Black Papers on Education*, London: Davis-Poynter.

Giddens, A. (1998) *The Third Way: The Renewal of Social Democracy*, London: Polity.

Harvey, D. (2005) *A Brief History of Neoliberalism*, Oxford: Oxford University Press.

Hayek, F. (2001) *The Road to Serfdom*, London: Routledge.

Heywood, A. (2003) *Political Ideologies: An Introduction*, 3rd edition, London: Palgrave Macmillan.

Hill, D. and Cole, M. (2004) *Schooling and Equality Fact, Concept and Policy*, London: Routledge.

Jones, K. (2003) *Education in Britain: 1944 to the Present*, London: Polity.

Knight, C. (1990) *The Making of Tory Education Policy in Post-war Britain 1950–1986*, Lewes: Falmer Press.

Kynaston, D. (2007) *Austerity Britain 1945–51*, London: Bloomsbury.

Lawton, D. (2005) *Education and the Labour Party Ideologies 1900–2001 and Beyond*, London: RoutledgeFalmer.

Olssen, M., Codd, J. and O'Neill, A.-M. (2004) *Education Policy – Globalisation, Citizenship and Democracy*, London: Sage.

Seldon, A. (2007) *Blair Unbound*, London: Simon & Schuster.

Simon, B. (1991) *Education and Social Order 1940–1990*, London: Lawrence and Wishart.

Tooley, J. (1997) 'Saving education from the "lurching steam roller": the democratic virtues of markets in education', in D. Bridges (ed.), *Education, Autonomy and Democratic Citizenship*, London: Routledge.

White, J. (1988) 'An Unconstitutional National Curriculum', in D. Lawton and C. Chitty (eds), *The National Curriculum, Bedford Way Paper 33*, London: Institute of Education, University of London.

Academies:
The privatization of education

Terry Wrigley

Chapter Outline

Introduction

I have a very good relationship with Andrew [Lord Adonis]. He rings me up and says, 'Do you want this school?' and I ask what it's like and if it sounds like the sort of place that we are interested in I say yes. (Lord Harris, June 2007)

This quotation neatly encapsulates the shift of power from elected public bodies to the private sector. Several years ago, you would have thought you were reading a science-fiction story. How could the future of a state-funded school be decided in such a subjective and self-interested manner?

It is not simply the initial establishment of academies, usually involving the closure of an existing school, which is at stake, but the power relationships under which they are then controlled. As lawyers have pointed out, education law, which regulates state schools, and provides important protection to parents, students and staff, is discarded once a school becomes an Academy (Anti-Academies Alliance 2007: 28–9). The sponsor has almost absolute powers, for example, appoint the headteacher and (after initial transfers) other staff, to determine who will be on its board of governors, the nature of the curriculum, the design of new buildings and policies on admissions and exclusions.

City academies were first proposed as a means to rescue 'seriously failing schools...breaking the cycle of underperformance and low expectations' (Blunkett, 2000). This is clearly no longer the case. Current plans are for 400, or about 1 in 10 English schools, and many of the schools which the government intend to close have received official recognition for their achievement and quality of education.

This chapter will examine various features of the Academies Programme, placing it within the context of a wider business agenda for education, including the growing resistance to them. It is inevitably partisan, as I have been personally involved in this campaign through research and speaking on public platforms. Readers wishing to read government claims in support of academies will find ample material via official websites.

Useful Websites

Websites that put forward the case for academies:

| Department for children, families and Schools Standards | www.standards.dfes.gov.uk/academies |
| Specialist Schools and Academies Trust | www.specialistschools.org.uk |

Websites that are critical of Academies:

| Anti-Academies Alliance | www.antiacademies.org.uk/ |
| Rethinking Education | www.rethinkinged.org.uk/index.html |

Activity

Read the Government information on academies and make notes.

1. To what extent does the information provided by the Government answer any of the criticisms in this chapter?

Origins

There are two main sources for the academies idea: City Technology Colleges (CTCs) in England (proposed by the Conservative government in 1986) and Charter Schools in the US (from 1991 onwards).

The CTCs were government-funded independent schools outside the control of local education authorities (LEAs). It was intended that private sector sponsors would make a substantial contribution towards the costs, and the curriculum would have a strong emphasis on technical scientific and practical subjects, business studies and design. The expected private sector contribution for each was about 8 million pounds towards building costs, though this failed to materialize. For many reasons, not solely financial, the concept was rejected by most major companies (Beckett, 2007: 3).

The preferred option, favoured by many within the Conservative Party, was a return to grammar schools and 11-plus selection, but was felt to be politically unpopular. Though the intention behind the CTCs is made clear by Kenneth Baker, Secretary of State for Education, who choose his words carefully when describing their admissions criteria: 'Pupils will span the full range of ability' but adding in the same breath 'They will be selected on the basis of their aptitude' (Beckett, 2007: 6). New Labour politicians have frequently used this neat and meaningless distinction to justify their current policies. Although CTCs in practice had to include some children from each 'ability' band, they were able to interview and select the children they thought would be easy to teach.

Jack Straw, Labour's education spokesman at that time, fiercely attacked the project as an 'expensive failure wasteful and wrong'. It has since emerged that even Kenneth Baker, the minister who introduced the idea, was personally opposed and that the Prime Minister Margaret Thatcher imposed it on him (Beckett, 2008). The intended target was to create one hundred CTCs but only fifteen actually opened, the last one in 1991.

Charter Schools

Charter Schools in the US began in 1991, and spread rapidly. In part, they were a response to demands for school reform from the teachers' union. They are publicly funded but legally autonomous, operating like independent businesses. They cannot charge tuition fees, have religious affiliations or select their students, but are free of some of the rules applying to other schools, and expected to be innovative in their teaching and curriculum. The result has been very mixed. On the one hand, the field was opened to large 'edu-businesses' (e.g. Edison which operates over one hundred schools in nineteen states). On the other, the Charter School reform provided new opportunities for groups of parents (often black or Hispanic) who were disillusioned with large high schools in which their children always seemed to fail, and has resulted in some progressive curriculum and teaching. Perhaps it was to avoid this latter possibility that Blair's Government set a requirement for a 2 million pounds contribution to building costs (albeit often unpaid).

Continuity with the CTC programme and academies can further be seen in the influential figure of Sir Cyril Taylor, who once headed the CTC Trust (under Margaret Thatcher) and later the Specialist Schools and Academies Trust (under Tony Blair). The leadership of both the Conservative and Labour Party supports the Academies project.

Privatization and school failure

Government ministers argue that academies are not a form of privatization. Their argument depends on a narrow interpretation of that word: for the present, at least, sponsors are not allowed to make a profit out of their schools. It is indeed true that they are funded almost entirely from the public purse, but so too is the arms industry. Academies are subject to some rules regarding admissions (a concession resulting from a major revolt by back-bench Labour MPs), but even private businesses are subject to some legal regulations.

In terms of control, they clearly are private, and regulated only through a funding agreement between the sponsor and a government minister. Indeed:

> Parents, pupils and most local authorities are kept well away from contract negotiations and seldom get to know what goes into them. (Anti-Academies Alliance, 2007: 28)

They form part of a wider strategy for transferring control of publicly funded schools, along with other public services such as health and council houses, to private control. The official explanation for this is that local authorities will commission but not control schools. Keith Mitchell, upon his retirement as Director of Education for Durham, spoke of the end of our public education system. He felt he had to speak out because so many of his colleagues in similar positions were bound to silence because of their positions, or through loyalty to the Labour Party (Mitchell, 2006). Education Secretary David Blunkett, on first announcing the academies, said quite plainly that they would be owned and run by sponsors (Blunkett, 2000).

It is still claimed that academies are a means of rescuing 'failing schools'. This claim is increasingly difficult to justify. Indeed, the grave problems encountered with the first two cohorts of academies (2002 and 2003 openers) have led the government to seize upon increasingly successful schools. Approximately 17 per cent of pupils at the schools closed to make way for the 2002 openers achieved five or more A*–C grades; the figure was 40 per cent for those opening in 2005, and 47 per cent for 2007. A notorious example is Islington Green School, serving a deprived area of Inner London; the school featured on a government poster in the shape of a Tube Map, highlighting London's most successful and improved schools – and in the same week was informed that it would be closed and converted into an Academy. In 2007, 35 per cent of its pupils gained five or more A*–C grades including English and maths, compared with 25 per cent average for all academies.

The government continues to use low achievement as a pretext for closure and privatization. Prime Minister Gordon Brown has placed schools with less than 30 per cent achieving five or more GCSEs at A*–Cs or equivalent with English and maths under threat. This is more likely, of course, in poorer areas, and affects around half the schools in major cities such as Birmingham and Liverpool. Ironically, this also includes most academies: perhaps they should be closed and transferred back into public control?

The impact of privatized control

The process of privatization has gathered pace in the past two decades, including basic public services such as schools, hospitals and council houses. In education, this began in the mid-1980s with school meals and cleaning being put out to tender, spread to support services such as careers advice or staff development, and reached a high point with major construction projects under the Private Finance Initiative (PFI, renamed Public Private Partnership or PPP in 2001). These have provided a bonanza for construction firms and banks that own new school buildings and land and rent them out to education authorities.

It is important to realize however that the Academies mark a qualitative change in the story of privatization, since they involve handing control of the education process itself into private hands. The Government's declared intention is that Academies, mainly urban and secondary will be followed by Trust Schools, which can be secondary, primary or special, and in any location.

It is important not to limit one's concept of privatization to directly making a profit. What is at stake is the changing purpose of education. As Ball argues in his book *The Education Debate*

> Within policy, education is now regarded primarily from an economic point of view. The social and economic purposes of education have been collapsed into a single, overriding emphasis on policy making for economic competitiveness and an increasing neglect or sidelining (other than in rhetoric) of the social purposes of education. (2008: 11–12)

Ball describes in great detail, in this and his earlier book *Education PLC* (2007), how much education policy has become dominated by issues of economic competitiveness within a global economy, which is understood in neo-liberal terms. Alan Sears (2003) argues that education is being pruned to match industrial needs, since broader school aims such as citizenship and culture are regarded as waste.

It is in this context that we can begin to understand the Education and Inspection Act (2006). One feature of the original Bill, namely admissions policy, attracted massive opposition, within and outside Parliament. Each individual academy was allowed to decide which children to admit, opening the gates for selection, but as a concession, the Government drew up rules forbidding interviews or selection by ability (though they can, as Specialist schools, admit 10 per cent on 'aptitude').

The Act, thus amended, was passed almost unnoticed, yet its other features were just as dangerous, if not more so. In effect, it divided the school population into two halves from age 14 onwards, an academic and a vocational track. The former will be entitled to a broad and balanced curriculum, including English, maths, science, a foreign language, history or geography, a design and technology subject, and one of the arts (including media). The latter, pursuing a work-related diploma, will receive a narrower and more functionalist version of the core (English, maths and science) and have no entitlement to a language, history or geography, design and technology, or the arts. This is both a deep incursion into the comprehensive school principle, and a shift in educational purpose – preparation for work, often low-skill low-paid jobs, will dominate.

It is important to emphasize that I am not arguing here against vocational subjects, but against them dominating the curriculum and dividing schools into two halves.

How are Academies run?

There is no simple answer to this, as each sponsor makes different decisions. The following section aims to explain some of the general problems. Where a specific illustration is given, it should not be assumed that this applies in all or even most cases, but the examples show the scope for misuse of power.

Governors

In other schools, staff representatives are elected by staff, parent representatives by parents, and education authority representatives are elected by either councillors or their nominees. In academies, the sponsor nominates almost all the governing body and can decide who will represent parents and teachers. This concentrates enormous power in the sponsor, who may use it inappropriately, making key educational decisions without adequate knowledge.

Staffing

Most staff are transferred, on their existing pay and conditions, from the predecessor school (i.e. the school closed to make way for the academy). However, the sponsor normally chooses a new head, and other staff as soon as anyone leaves. Pay and conditions can be set regardless of national norms or trade union agreements. There are many cases of teachers having to work longer hours, or finding that the sponsor will not recognize their union. Many Academies have suffered high levels of staff turnover, including heads, resulting in instability and inexperience. Some have appointed headteachers on ideological or religious grounds who do not have sufficient experience of inner-city schools (e.g. Beckett, 2007: 93).

Religious sponsors can discriminate when appointing staff, even when the school is nominally secular. An extreme case occurred at Kings Academy in Middlesbrough:

> Instead of being asked about teaching style he was quizzed on his views on birth control and whether or not he believed in Noah's Ark.... 'I was cut short by a sarcastic and disturbing comment – What's the point of sending young people out into the world with 20 GCSEs when they're going to Hell?' [The interviewee complaining about this treatment was not anti-religion: he was himself a Methodist lay preacher!]. (Anti-Academies Alliance, 2007: 24)

Buildings

Given the sponsors' power, they have been able to make architectural decisions, which might be more suitable to a city office or car salesroom than to a school. Architects have been appointed without any school design experience, and often impractical and very expensive buildings are built as monuments to the sponsor's ego. Academies have cost the taxpayer far more than other schools, despite the sponsor's contribution.

Many academies look impressive but cold: shiny steel and glass surfaces, grey and brown colour schemes, and balconies and spaces which appear designed for surveillance, with few quiet places to sit, relax and work collaborative other than at computers. Some look like a cross between a battleship, a prison and a call centre.

Bexley's sponsor commissioned Sir Norman Foster's practice, which had never designed a school before as the architects. He decided on an open plan: the classrooms had no fourth wall! This had to be filled in later, at further expense to the taxpayer. Even Sir Cyril Taylor at the Specialist Schools and Academies Trust had to admit in a *Guardian* interview that the building side of things had been a complete nightmare (Anti-Academies Alliance, 2007: 20). It has cost taxpayers an additional 15 million pounds to put right faults in five academies. In one case, a nearly new sports hall was demolished and rebuilt, at a cost of 1 million pounds, so that it could charge for community use while avoiding VAT (National Audit Office, 2007).

The Peterborough Academy was built without a playground or recreational space. When reporters challenged the head, he replied that the students wouldn't need it because they wouldn't have any recreational time either – but they would be able to drink water during lessons!

Finance

The original requirement was for the sponsor to subsidize construction costs by 2 million pounds; this figure was soon dwarfed by the additional building costs compared with normal schools, which taxpayers have to pay. In practice, this 2 million pounds was often reduced as few benefactors stepped forward. Soon they were being offered three academies for the price of two. There was a scandal when a journalist discovered potential sponsors being offered knighthoods and even seats in the House of Lords (Beckett, 2007: 28). After this, even fewer donors stepped forward. Thus Academies were no longer seen as an asset to the sponsors in promoting their interests in the media. Eventually a formal decision was reached that sponsors could offer support in kind over a number of years rather than cash down.

Sponsors clearly have a variety of motives, from religious zeal or status to a more general desire to make education more business oriented. Some have used the rhetoric of philanthropy – hyper-rich people putting something back. This rebounded in the case of ARK (Absolute Return for Kids), a charity run by millionaire merchant bankers and hedge fund speculators, when they tried to take over Islington Green School. First on the list of this organization's sponsors is a hedge fund based in the tax haven of the Cayman Islands. Ken Muller, National Union of Teachers (NUT) representative at the school, confronted ARK publicly: If you really want to help our school, pay your taxes! (See Beckett, 2007: 103seq. and Muller, 2008 for further details.)

Taxpayers fund all of the running costs of the school after initial construction, yet they have no say in how the money is used. This includes an extra 1,600 pounds per pupil for resources as a start-up fund, even though the academy inherits the assets of the predecessor school. The Department of Children, Schools and Families (DCSF) have also sent in large numbers of consultants to advise the schools how to raise their test scores quickly, which reveals perhaps how slight and uncertain the sponsors' educational contribution has been. In 2005, the House of Commons Select Committee for Education and Skills calculated that the average cost of educating a child in an academy was 21,000 pounds compared with 14,000 pounds in the maintained sector. The National Audit Office report (2007) highlighted that the Excellence in Cities programmes was cheaper and more effective in improving education in inner-city schools (Anti-Academies Alliance, 2007: 19–20).

Admissions and exclusions

The original pretext for setting up Academies was to improve education for extremely deprived inner-city communities. It soon became apparent that many sponsors and headteachers were working hard, even deviously, to re-engineer the school population. This can occur in various ways: the attractions of a brand new building and all the publicity, excluding more difficult pupils, and within the limit of the law through their admissions policies. Overall there has been a substantial reduction in the proportion of pupils on free school meals, a poverty indicator, compared with the predecessor schools. Academies are also able to refuse pupils with special educational needs (SEN), unless their Statement specifically mentions that school, though some heads have upheld an inclusive admissions policy. Many stories emerged from witnesses from local campaign groups to the MPs Committee of Enquiry (Anti-Academies Alliance, 2007):

1. King's Academy, Middlesborough, expelled twenty-seven pupils in its first year, compared with ten in total by the seven maintained schools in the local authority. Unlike maintained schools, there is no independent appeal body. A further ten pupils at Kings were withdrawn by their parents under threat of exclusion.
2. In some cases, it is suspected that very strict disciplinary codes have been introduced in order to identify and drive out less compliant pupils. Parents at the Trinity Academy, Doncaster, were so outraged that a protest meeting attracted over two hundred; some pupils with good behaviour records had suddenly found themselves in 7 hours detention a week once the academy opened.
3. Walsall Academy reduced the percentage of pupils on free meals from 51 per cent to 11 per cent. This was partly achieved by telling parents that their children would not benefit from the school unless they had broadband internet access. The cost of uniform was also a deterrent: the sports kit alone costs 120 pounds.
4. Given where academies are located and the high levels of poverty, local children tend towards below average attainment. Some academies use so-called fair banding to achieve a national average balance, which is untypical of the local area. Bands A–D are defined such that each matches a quarter of the national population. If only 10 per cent of local children are in the top band and 40 per cent are in the bottom band, recruiting 25 per cent into each will exclude many poorer local children and bring in higher attaining pupils from further away. Mossbourn in Hackney also

requires prospective parents to bring their child to be tested a year in advance, further deterring the less informed or more troubled families.

A delegation from Newcastle told the enquiry that the sponsor, Lord Laidlaw, a resident of Monte Carlo who has avoided paying UK taxes for over 20 years, wanted to relocate the new school nearer to new, more upmarket housing, presumably with a view to attracting more upmarket pupils. No provision had been made at the new Academy for English as an Additional Language or for SEN. Governors of a school in Waltham Forest were told that sponsorship was based on a condition – none of the children from the predecessor school could attend!

Changing schools, changing pupils

Some academy heads insist on providing for local children just like their predecessor school, but given the pressure for rapidly improving results, the temptation is strong to re-engineer the population. This obviously has an impact on neighbouring schools. The nearest school to Bexley Business Academy saw its percentage of SEN pupils rise from 44 to 53 per cent. In Sandwell, historically 90 per cent of parents got their first choice of secondary school, but this dropped to 71 per cent when the Academy opened.

Religious sponsorship may also create barriers. Some schools which were secular comprehensives serving their local area, are now, if not overtly faith schools, sponsored by individuals or organizations with strong religious beliefs. They can use church membership as a criterion when admitting pupils. For example, the secular comprehensive school in Merton, which was taken over by the Church of England, charity Toc H and the Centre for British Teachers Education Trust (CfBT) edu-business was allowed to select up to a third of its pupils on the basis of church membership.

Improving the quality of education?

The Blair government rushed headlong into the Academies project, but then desperately needed evidence to justify its decision retrospectively. The target of 200 academies was announced even before the first 3 academies had pupils sitting GCSEs who had been at their new school throughout Key Stage 4. They soon got into the situation of creating 'policy-based evidence' rather than 'evidence-based policy'.

Almost immediately, the government's media machine, led by Lord Adonis, announced miraculous improvements in GCSE results. However, it soon became apparent that the Academies were being strongly advised to enter pupils for General National Vocational Qualification (GNVQ). A recent decision had been made that a GNVQ Intermediate pass would be counted as equivalent to four A*–C grades at GCSE. Therefore a pupil passing GNVQ and gaining a C in any other subject would count as having jumped the magic hurdle of five A*–Cs or the equivalent. The number of GNVQ entries was 13 times as high as at the predecessor schools. Pupils could also repeat the GNVQ assessment tasks and tests until they passed them.

Reasons for equivalence

Neither Ofsted nor Qualifications and Curriculum Authority (QCA) could provide any justification for this supposed equivalence. Some Academy pupils were taking three or more GNVQs as well as a range of other subjects, so they clearly weren't the equivalent of four GCSE subjects; these pupils would have been working throughout the night. In 2004, by recounting each GNVQ as equal to only one rather than to four C grades, it became clear that there was little improvement on the predecessor schools.

There was also the issue of quality. Large numbers of pupils passing GNVQ Intermediate were gaining D and E grades in most other subjects. Over 90 per cent of pupils with a C or higher in GCSE Science also gained a C or above in maths, but only half those passing GNVQ Intermediate in Science got C or above in maths. Similar results emerged when comparing Information Communication Technology (ICT) and maths. It seems a fair conclusion that, at its margins, a GNVQ Intermediate is equal to an E not a C. Indeed, Filton FE College in Bristol only counts a Merit or Distinction as equivalent to a C, and then only as a single subject. The GNVQ has since been phased out.

Real improvement?

By 2006, following widespread media attention as other lower-achieving schools were claiming miraculous improvement through using the GNVQ, the Government were forced to adopt a new measure: the five A*–Cs or equivalent had to include English and maths. In other words, at the lower margins, a school can count a GNVQ Intermediate plus a C in English and in maths. Three subjects are still narrow, as a school leaving certificate, but provides a more reliable comparison between schools.

Applying this new official criterion, and comparing with their predecessors' results in 2002, just before the first academies opened, the academies had made a gain of 8 percentage points from 14 to 22 per cent. However, all schools nationally had improved 4 percentage points in that period, so the net benefit of becoming Academies was only 4 percentage points (Anti-Academies Alliance, 2007: 45–6). This is a very small increase, given the high construction and other costs (see above) and the lower proportion of poorer students. Meanwhile, the government continued to spin to the media the story that the percentage gaining five A*–Cs had doubled (i.e. they used the old criterion, neglecting to explain about the phoney GNVQ equivalence or that this didn't require English and maths).

Even this was at the price of a considerable curriculum narrowing, as Academies were driven towards quick-fix improvements in results. Looking only at their relatively successful pupils (i.e. the 42 per cent gaining five A*–Cs or equivalent, regardless of English and maths):

- only two-thirds achieved C or above in English (ditto maths)
- around half achieved this level in science
- only a quarter achieved C or above in history or geography
- only a quarter gained C or above in a language (indeed, only two-thirds of these relatively successful pupils even studied a language at Key Stage 4)
- there was a massive increase in GNVQ entries (more than one entry per pupil on average) but these were almost all in science and ICT, that is, replacing existing GCSEs rather than introducing new vocational choices (Anti-Academies Alliance, 2007: 47).

Breadth of curriculum was being sacrificed to quick-fix tactics to demonstrate success: these pupils would not count as well-educated school leavers elsewhere in Europe. Ironically too, given the policy orientation referred to earlier, the academies were not even providing what the Confederation of British Industry were demanding, that is, success in core skills of literacy and numeracy, and improved vocational preparation.

In 2007, the proportion jumping the new hurdle (five A*–C or equivalent including English and maths) rose, but the academies' student population was changing dramatically by this time. Many academies have reduced the proportion of pupils on free school meals; many have drawn in large numbers of pupils who would have attended other schools; some appear to have lost a significant number of pupils between Key Stage 3 tests and GCSE, whether by expulsion or by removing them from the data.

Even without taking this population change into account, official statistical analyses show a gain (on five or more A*–Cs or equivalent with English and maths) of only 10.3 percentage points between 2002 and 2007. Since all schools gained by 6.4 percentage points over that time, there has been only a small value added as a result of conversion to academies of around 4 percentage points. After adjusting for the population change, the net gain is almost zero.

The future

The government, now with Gordon Brown as Prime Minister, is evidently embarrassed by the serious problems of the Academies Programme, yet feels unable to abandon it. Brown announced an enquiry, but in secret and without the opportunity for opponents to present evidence. Partly this is because Brown is a firm believer in neo-liberal policies, including privatization of public services. Andrew Adonis, for many years the power behind the throne but recently promoted to Lord Adonis in order to become official School Minister, continues to boast of the academies' achievement.

Meanwhile, opposition across England grows with each expansion of the project. Some of the campaigns have been extremely creative and effective, uniting teachers and parents.

For instance, car dealer Reg Vardy was driven away from one school he attempted to take over in a mining village near to Doncaster; staff and parents (1) advertised the school for sale on eBay; (2) held a mock car sale in the school playground; (3) put up banners saying 'they closed our pit and took away our jobs, they're not taking our school'. Islington Green staff borrowed costumes from a fancy dress shop to demonstrate as Fat Cats outside the city offices of their potential sponsors.

Some academies have chronic problems. The first three (Bexley, Greig and Unity, opened in 2002) have had very critical inspection reports. (This embarrassment is unlikely to be repeated with others, however, since Ofsted now has a carefully monitored team to inspect Academies.)

Intense campaigning at local and national levels, as well as bad publicity, has forced a rethink about sponsors. Some have clearly proved an embarrassment to government, and there has been a dearth of high-technology companies with something to offer of educational value. The Government's strategy is now oriented towards the Church of England and universities. The former has been promised 100 additional secondary schools, as academies, which shifts the balance substantially towards church schools in urban areas. This is highly questionable in terms of that other Government aim, of fostering greater ethnic integration and community cohesion. There has, at the time of writing, been little or no enthusiasm from universities, though some have signed up which have little or no school experience. The Government are understandably anxious to avoid a reputation of failure. It is significant that, as stated above, increasingly successful schools are being earmarked for closure and conversion into academies.

The industrial focus of Academies

Almost all the early academies had either a Business and Enterprise or a Computing specialism. This remains the dominant pattern, and clearly Academies have a role to play in the wider shift in the aims and orientation of English secondary education referred to above. Some local authorities, seizing on the perceived desperation of the Government, have gained agreement that they can themselves become sponsors of their current schools, as academies. However, the pattern is generally that they become co-sponsors with commercial companies. Shortly after Sunderland announced that it would become joint sponsor of three of its own schools, one of its partners announced that they were installing a practice call centre in one in order to 'raise the pupils' aspirations'. Manchester's co-sponsored academies will each specialize in preparing pupils for employment in a specific industry or commercial activity. One co-sponsor, Manchester Airport, has openly stated that the principle purpose of its Academy will be to provide employees for the airport. How, one wonders, will the city's 11-year-olds choose their secondary schools: 'Please mummy can I go to the Travel and Tourism Academy, so that I can become a baggage handler when I grow up' (see Titcombe, 2008: 56 for further information).

Popularity of Academies

Lord Adonis continues to claim that the academies are very popular with parents. It is hardly surprising, given the new buildings and the publicity hype about improved results, that many receive large numbers of applicants. There is also substantial opposition almost anywhere academies are proposed. The record of consultation is a known scandal, with parents denied key facts. Witnesses to the House of Commons enquiry repeatedly brought stories of manipulation and falsification:

> The academy proposals were accompanied by a vast amount of spin. The consultation documents were not balanced consultations seeking to elicit genuine views and opinions – they were more like sales-pitches full of glitzy photographs of pupils in public schools. More like something an expensive advertising agency would produce. (Delegation from Oxford, see Anti-Academies Alliance, 2007: 30–1)

Siobhain Mcdonagh MP, a New Labour loyalist, sent a questionnaire to parents, with the following choice of boxes to tick:

- Yes, I am in favour of raising standards at Mitcham Vale and Tamworth Manor High School by getting Academy status.
- No, I am against these changes to Mitcham Vale and Tamworth Manor High Schools designed to improve examination standards (ibid.).

If Academies were as popular and successful as claimed, the Government would not have to blackmail local authorities into handing over local schools. That is effectively what is happening: councils must demonstrate that they have seriously considered academies, and receive strong indications that they will not get any new school buildings unless they hand over some schools.

> Newcastle's Councillors do not want an academy. In fact, the Liberal Democrat council was elected specifically on a platform of not having one. They have made no secret of the reason they changed their minds. Building Schools for the Future money was tied to the academy. If they denied the Government its academy, they would get no money for the city's schools. If they agreed, they could have £200 million. Councillor Nick Cott said: 'It's not just the academy that rests on that but the funding for the BSF project.' (Beckett, 2007: 116)

Nevertheless, a few local authorities have succeeded in defying these threats.

One difficult question is the relationship of academies to the local community and other schools. The National Audit Office Report (2007) itself highlighted a failure of academies to benefit local community services or work with neighbouring schools. In the beginning, it was assumed by many that the academies were to become a new kind of grammar school selecting higher achievers. The emerging picture is more varied. Some have tried this but failed, being unable to compete against schools with well-established reputations including grammar and church schools. In other cases, academies are being customized towards a struggling council estate, and will probably provide a low level of education akin to the post-1944 secondary modern schools. One common factor, however, is the strong business orientation.

Resistance is growing, and in addition to the many local campaign groups, the major teacher trade unions and others such as Unison have affiliated to the Anti-Academies Alliance. The problems with the programme will not disappear once more academies have opened, but are likely to become even more evident, as sponsors unduly assert their autonomy, the curriculum is distorted, greater segregation (social class, ethnic and religious) arises, neighbouring schools are disadvantaged, and in some cases religious fervour leads to increasingly disciplinarian regimes.

Conclusion

This chapter began by locating the academies within a wider context of privatization, both in the sense of controlling the school and in terms of educational purpose. It is important to bear this context in mind when considering the development of resistance. We are living in a world marked by deep crisis: environment (climate chaos), poverty (at home and globally) and war. It is increasingly apparent that these crises are rooted in the economic and political structure of capitalism – the concentration of power in the hands of the global hyper-rich, who in their greed for profit appear ready to sacrifice even the earth itself (see Wrigley, 2006).

> Its owners treat the planet as if it could be discarded, a commodity to be used up.... But what other world are we going to move to? Are we all obliged to swallow the line that god sold the planet to a few companies because in a foul mood he decided to privatise the universe. (Galeano, 2000)

Schools must not be limited to serving only economic goals, and neglecting other educational aims such as personal and cultural development and global citizenship. The struggle against academies is part of a wider struggle to save public education.

Key Points

- Academies represent a fundamental change in the nature of secondary education provision
- Academies represent the effective privatization of the school system
- The nature of the privatization that Academies represent goes further than previous privatization policies in that business now controls the process of education
- Sponsors (owners) of academies have control over the nature of the curriculum provided, school policies, admissions and exclusions
- The development of the academies initiative draws on previous Conservative policies such as CTCs and the Charter School movement in the US
- Academies do not address the educational needs of the pupils it is claimed they have been set up to aid
- Evidence of the success of Academies in reaching government targets is questionable
- There is an increased role for religious organizations in the school system through the Academies programme.

Further Reading

Martin Allen and Patrick Ainley (2007) *Education Make You Fick, Innit?*, London: Tufnell Press.

Stephen Ball (2007) *Education PLC: Understanding Private Sector Participation in Public Sector Education*, London: Routledge.

Francis Beckett (2007) *The Great City Academy Fraud*, London: Continuum.

Hugh Lauder and David Hughes (1999) *Trading Futures: Why Markets in Education Don't Work*, Maidenhead: Open University Press.

References

Anti-Academies Alliance (2007) *Report on the MPs Committee of Enquiry into Academies and Trust Schools*, 12 June 2007, Palace of Westminster (www.antiacademies.org.uk).

Ball, S. (2007) *Education PLC*, London: Routledge.

Ball, S. (2008) *The Education Debate*, Bristol: Policy Press.

Beckett, F. (2007) *The Great City Academy Fraud*, London: Continuum.

Beckett, F. (2008) *We Pay the Piper – They Call the Tune*, London: Anti-Academies Alliance.

Blunkett, D. (2000) *Speech Delivered to the Social Market Foundation*, 15 March (www.dfes.gov.uk/speeches).

Galeano, E. (2000) *Upside Down: A Primer for the Looking-Glass World*, New York: Metropolitan Books.

Harris, Lord (2007) Interview in *Financial Times*, 19 June. (See parliamentary question by Ken Purchase MP, Daily Hansard 20 June 2007.)

Mitchell K. (2006) 'Report of his retirement speech', *Guardian*, 10 April (http://education.guardian.co.uk/policy/story/0,,1750884,00.html).

Muller, K. (2008) 'Hey! Bankers! Leave those kids alone: the fight to save Islington Green School', *Forum* 50(1), pp. 71–84.

National Audit Office (2007) *The Academies Programme*.

Sears A. (2003) *Retooling the Mind Factory: Education in a Lean State*, Aurora, ON: Garamond Press.

Titcombe, R. (2008) 'How Academies threaten the comprehensive curriculum', *Forum* 50(1), pp. 49–60.

Wrigley (2006) *Another School is Possible*, London: Bookmarks.

3 Standards, testing and reality

Kate MacDonald

Introduction

On Monday 19 May 2008 the BBC investigative programme *Panorama* ran an episode titled 'Tested to Destruction'. The following day a Select Committee report argued that the testing regime in England had become excessive (Curtis, 2008). These criticisms are the most recent of a series of concerns about how the testing and standards regime have developed since the introduction of the National Curriculum. Testing was introduced in the nineteenth century in the pursuit of equity through merit and open competition (Black, 1998a). The idea, that a fair tool could be invented which would allow selection of talent for the civil service, was viewed both as a modern and just technique which would produce equal access (ibid.). This idea of testing was sustained through the pursuit of intelligence testing in the mid-twentieth century and into what Broadfoot (2000) describes as a multimillion pound modern industry which claims transparency and equity and which has grown substantially during the past 30 years. In this twentieth-century version, testing offers to assess pupil performance and future potential. While its principle purpose is to discriminate between pupils, it is also used to indicate the standards of the school, as well as those of teachers. In the nineteenth century the payment by results system, which distributed funding according to outcomes in the emerging elementary school system had a negative effect on the curriculum (Green, 1990). As it was used to discipline teachers, their main motivation became a fear of failure rather than engaging the interest and motivation of pupils (Black, 1998b). As the payment by results system illustrates, it is also the case that the testing regime can alter both the status and motivation of teachers, as well as shape the curriculum and practices within school. Testing involves social reproduction, legitimation of particular forms of knowledge and social control (Filer, 2000). It is these consequences that this chapter aims to examine after a brief exploration of the technical claims of testing itself.

Testing technology

Testing in the English system came to prominence as a means of selecting an elite; that is, it provided an apparently meritocratic and fair way of distributing scarce resources, for example, jobs in the civil service. A key feature of this form of testing is the assumption that the majority should fail to achieve certification or entrance. Thus, certification itself becomes a commodity that can be traded in for access to work and higher education and becomes a symbol of the status of the individual, not least because, the test is seen as legitimate by those who fail. In addition, it was argued that schools and teachers could be judged on their results in, for example, GCSE and A level. This type of testing differs from that of mass testing currently used to assert the National Curriculum standards, which are claimed to provide a broader view of achievement in the school system. Mass testing is used to certify competence in individuals and to evaluate the effectiveness of teachers and schools for all pupils against an external benchmark. Contemporary concerns about standards and testing can be divided into four key areas: who controls the system; what are its purposes; what knowledge and skills are to be tested; how the outcomes are expressed and used.

Control of testing

The control of selective testing in England was once the province of the universities who tested to select entrants and then set national standards of certification. However, government demands for accountability led to greater certification and the arrival of a nationally defined curriculum resulting in a range of systems. Black (1998a) identifies five parallel systems of testing in England. These are standardized tests for diagnostic purposes – (mainly commercially produced). National Curriculum assessment at seven, eleven, fourteen – supposedly based on a national average which is contracted to public examination groups and compulsory for schools. Then there are GCSE bodies, vocational and occupational selection linked to training bodies, and, finally, teacher assessment. Each of these systems has a set of purposes, means of implementation and record of outcomes. In England, increasing emphasis has been placed on external tests as a measure of the efficiency of the system and pupil achievement, thus making testing high stakes. High-stakes testing occurs where the test has significant outcomes, either for pupils or teachers (Jones et al., 2003). At the same time teacher-led formative assessment has declined despite evidence that it is both useful and valid for assessment and learning (Harlen, 2005; Black et al., 2003; William, 2000). A similar pattern in the US of state mandated tests, has led to an increase in single source high-stake testing (Abrams and Madaus, 2003) and a pressure to lower costs (Clarke et al., 2000), so that the state can provide a simple and single measurement for which both the school and its pupils are accountable.

The purpose of testing

In England, the purpose of testing in the school system has become viewed more strongly as an agent of economic regeneration and as a measure of school and teacher efficiency. The pressure to evidence a numerate and literate workforce has grown from Conservative policy, involving performance measurement of schools as a means to encourage competition (Shaw, 2000), to Prime Minister Blair using the raising of national scores as an incentive to international investment (Wrigley, 2006). As a result, tests have become multi-purpose, informing both measures of national, school and individual performance and parental choice. However, the fitness for purpose of these figures has been called into question (Black, 1998a), as has the authenticity and truthfulness of the test in reporting school achievement (Gewirtz, 2000). The desire of politicians to produce a single figure measurement which can easily be understood throws into doubt the validity of a figure, since figures are achieved by aggregating data (Davis, 1998). Whether this represents anything meaningful or has a useful relationship to knowledge and skills is questionable (Brown et al., 2003). William (2003: 105) argues that the system has taken a 'wrong turn' in using tests, designed to select and certify, as a means to make institutions accountable because assessment is no longer linked to the learning process but to evaluative statements about teachers and schools.

Forms of testing

Forms of testing are important when defining both the type of testing and the range of knowledge and skills to be tested. There is a tension between the external purpose of testing which results in public certification and evaluation and the testing used in support of learning, that is, formative assessment. Formative assessment is part of the process of learning and involves a dialogue between learner and teacher. Examinations and summative work place more emphasis on outcomes and certification of student and teacher performance. Gipps (1995) argues that this tradition of testing is built upon an idea that knowledge could be broken into sequences of component parts which could function independently. Similarly, skills could be divided in order of complexity. Learning was viewed both as linear and progressive and it was assumed that context played little part, thus making 'scientific' testing a real possibility. It was understood that the construction of tests that were both reliable and valid would enable comparisons of the system at a number of levels. It was also recognized that the emphasis on reliability compromised validity, and in the process promoted the value of certification over the content and style of learning. More recently, this view has been challenged by the 'Constructivist' account of learning which emphasizes processes of reconstructing and revisiting knowledge in which making sense to the learner is a significant element. Meta cognition is an important part of real learning as opposed to, or rather than, any abstract capacity to manipulate (Davis, 1998). Teacher-based formative tests which endeavour to recognize this more complex version of learning, and a wider scope of what counts as knowledge in real world situations, were initially devised through the Assessment of Performance Unit alongside the introduction of the Key Stage assessments, but were quickly abandoned as being too expensive, complex and insufficiently reliable (Black, 1998a). Also of significance, is the evidence that testing itself is antithetical to motivation and learning for a number of pupils (Hickey and Zuiker, 2005), and thus challenges the view that an increase in testing will raise standards.

The hidden issues in testing

One of the complexities, hidden by this national debate about standards, is the issue of how well tests represent the ideas and skills of the subject. The pursuit of single score tests is achieved at the cost of limiting the content and format of testing. Since the 1960s, among educationalists, a different form of testing based on educational rather than psychometric ideas has been promoted. These criterion tests, which measure the degree of competence attained by a student, aim to produce a better and fairer measurement of achievement in a subject. By doing so, they are said to allow for a broader area of the subject to be explored and for the context to be part of the testing process (Black, 1998a; Broadfoot and Pollard, 2000). The view of teachers is that teacher tests are more likely to reflect the nature of the subject (Harlen, 2005) than external tests which tend to be more concerned with reliability (Gipps, 1995). However, these objectives sit uneasily with the assertions made by politicians that summative test results are external, reliable and comparative and that testing does in fact raise standards. While refusing to incorporate formative assessment, neither the government nor the examination boards have published statistics on the reliability of external testing (William, 2003).

Validity, reliability and tests – high stakes

High-stake tests which inform decisions of social significance tend to be expressed in simple numbers or levels achieved by aggregating a number of scores. At best, these numbers represent a sample rather than any sense of 'full performance' of pupils' knowledge and understanding (Abrams and Madaus, 2003). As early as 1998, Chris Woodhead expressed concerns about the reliability of national Key Stage testing, suggesting that they were not necessarily 'right' and that meaningful comparison was simply not possible due to the frequency with which they were being changed (Woodhead, 1998). More recently, teachers have drawn attention to the inconsistency between Key Stage 2 and 3 tests, as an accurate measure of progress (Sinnot, 2005). In 1995, Gipps pointed out that testers had principally been concerned with issues of prediction, construct and content and not whether tests were adequate and appropriate in order to draw inferences. Making a similar observation, Filer (2000) indicates that the main issue with testing is to separate the technical aspect from the social functions of reproduction, legitimation of knowledge and social control, and to acknowledge the limitations of the former (i.e. the technical). Despite these concerns, however, over the past 20 years the English system of education has increasingly subscribed to the agenda of externally constructed and validated tests, by limiting elements of GCSE coursework (Stewart and Mansell, 2006) and focusing upon a narrower regime of Key Stage testing, thus equating assessment with high-stake tests. The consequences of this both on teachers and pupils will now be explored.

Activity

Black (1998a) identifies four ways of describing a pupil's performance:

- Fourth in the class in arithmetic
- Can add pairs of two digit numbers
- Has achieved basic competence in arithmetic
- Has reached level four in arithmetic

1. Are any of these measures (a) reliable or (b) valid?
2. Which is the most useful measure of achievement to: (a) pupils, (b) teachers, (c) a potential employer, (d) to an inspector concerned with the school standards?

Teachers

Discussion of the role of the teacher before 1988 often focused on the breadth of the pedagogical role. This explored whether teaching amounted to an emerging profession defined by the capacity for teachers to be autonomous decision makers, with a diffuse sense of responsibility, both in and out of the classroom. The abolition of the 11-plus examination, in many areas, had left primary school teachers with greater freedom than before (Pollard et al., 1994). Teachers had been encouraged to become engaged in the design, development and assessment of the curriculum, extending the idea of their professional competence beyond classroom pedagogy to give them opportunities to legitimate knowledge and make decisions about pupil competence (Black, 1998a). Consequently, teachers became not only concerned with classroom activities, but with the personal and moral development of pupils.

Accountability and control

The 1988 Education Reform Act (ERA) subjected teachers to a greater level of control than had existed since the nineteenth century (Broadfoot and Pollard, 2000). The keen emphasis on measurable performance, of pupils, teachers and schools, gave much greater prominence to the outcomes of testing. As Apple (2004: 197) suggests, it puts 'price tags on schools'. The emphasis on testing in a nationally devised framework brought a direct challenge to those teachers who viewed the child as the centre of the school. National policy gave priority to effective schools whose success was measured and used in a variety of contexts to claim improvement and success (Docking, 2000). Teachers were no longer viewed as having a broad professional competence. Instead, they were simply required to comply with externally devised and validated schemes. This produced the effect of reducing teacher autonomy over the content of the curriculum, the criteria for assessment and the definition of appropriate academic standards. Increased emphasis was thus placed on delivery (Coffey, 2001). Teachers as individuals retained their sense of selves as extended professionals; their formal role was to remain accountable for the classroom and measurement of pupil learning. For the primary school teacher this involved a change from an extended to a restricted professional role (Pollard et al., 1994). Broadfoot and Pollard (2000: 18) suggest that teachers moved from a 'covenant to a contract work ethic'. While some retained a personal sense of accountability and acquired new expertise within their role and through the curriculum, others felt less able to deliver under externally measured performance criteria. This switch, to performance measurement rather than competence, is one which allowed for greater external control over teachers and classroom pedagogy. For example, the report on Leeds primary schools further reinforced this perspective, suggesting that teachers lacked focus on pupil learning and had been misled in their commitment to child-centred learning. This added strength to the search by Ofsted for best practice in the form of direct teaching, mixed teaching strategies and ability grouping (Alexander, 1997) and reinforced the view that teachers were no longer competent to make judgements either in or out of the classroom. These pressures were reflected in debate regarding the modernization of the teaching profession, which introduced links between appraisal standards, pay and reform of the workforce (Tomlinson, 2003). Although contested by the teacher unions (Wrigley, 2006), the overall outcome has been a more heavily monitored and controlled workforce, in which claims to extended professionalism have been severely circumscribed.

Policy without evidence

Despite research evidence that external factors of class, parental interest, teacher status and peer pressure are more influential in determining pupil test scores, the far-reaching impact of international comparisons of test results has prompted the advocacy of an East European model of pedagogy. Commenting on the link between such international comparisons and the introduction of the numeracy strategy, for example, Elliott and Hufton (2000) note that there was clear recognition that cultural factors, external to the school, influenced test scores. Nevertheless, the perceived 'need' to reform curriculum practices has led to the adoption of centrally defined pedagogies, as a key feature of the numeracy and literacy strategies. Thus, while some teachers had built their own pedagogy on learning theory, by adopting the idea of working within the zone of proximal development for individual children (Gipps, 1995), increasingly the literacy strategy has come to be defined as *the* pedagogy believed to produce the highest and most favourable results (Mroz et al., 2000). Indeed, English et al.'s (2002) work has identified a tension between short-term objectives and teaching for the long term and concludes that teaching for understanding has become an 'optional extra' (ibid.: 22) against the goal of interactivity. This has resulted in little opportunity for the development of complex and elaborate ideas. Teachers' concerns, about their accountability to parents and the impact of Ofsted, weigh more heavily than their pedagogical principles of developing extended interaction with pupils. Smith et al. (2004) suggest that although the impact on interaction in the classroom during teaching has not been 'dramatically' changed, there is now more teacher direction in numeracy, where as a consequence the majority of questions have become lower order. Teachers prompt for the required answers and rarely give assistance in finding more complex ones.

The importance of formative assessment

Despite evidence that formative assessment can raise standards through a dialogue between pupils and teachers (Black et al., 2003; William, 2003), this has been largely ignored. Formative assessment has declined and teachers now focus on the content of high-stake tests. The judgement of teachers, about the link between assessment and learning, has been undermined by change in the style and control of assessment associated with the National Curriculum. In England, teacher judgements have become identified with formative rather than summative forms of assessment, although this is not the case in other parts of the world (Harlen, 2005). This lack of trust can be traced back to 1992, when the government challenged the reliability of the teacher-assessed component of GCSE. This was followed by the rejection of the Task Group on Assessment and Testing's (TGAT) recommendation that teacher judgement should be part of the frame of all Key Stages tests (James, 2000). William (2001, 2003) and Harlen (2005) challenge the view that teacher judgements are intrinsically less valid than those produced by external forms of assessment. Both also suggest that if the resources put into developing an external system had been used to develop teacher assessment skills, then the assessment system could surely have incorporated teacher summative judgement and retained a more effective way of learning for pupils. This tension is finally coming to attention. Sheerman (2008, cited in Curtis, 2008) chairman of the government Select Committee stated 'It's a call for a proper balance between testing and learning. We have examined the effect of testing forensically and now we need to rethink and to trust teachers more than we do.' Whether this is reflected in future policy remains to be seen.

Demands on teachers

As teachers respond to the demands of external criteria they inevitably change their priorities. As early as 1994, Pollard et al. (1994) noted teachers' concerns about working to a checklist. The National Union of Teachers (NUT) (Sinnot, 2005) has argued that the impact of Key Stage tests is that teachers now teach to the test, thus narrowing the breadth of the curriculum. As noted earlier, the lack of consistency between Key Stage 2 and 3 has made the task of diagnosing or advising pupils difficult. Overall, the effects of putting a premium on performance has been to make less time available to consider the whole child and to show that teachers no longer have a stake in the system, but are merely contracted to meet nationally set goals (James, 2000).

Gewirtz (2000) suggests that the model of accountability adopted by the English system, of performance and external auditing, results in compliance to routines and standards. This has driven out teachers' capacity to deliver diversity, creativity and autonomy. Roscoe (2007) expressed a similar view in a study of biology teachers in which he argues that they have made a sleep walk into a test culture with the consequence of stifling creativity. Teachers now concentrate on curriculum content and train pupils to practice answering questions, which results in a transmission-based pedagogy that is test focused, rather than learning orientated (Harlen, 2005).

The impact on testing

In commentaries on the impact of assessment on teacher training, Furlong (2005) and Tomlinson (2003) argue that the government is no longer interested in the notion of an individual professional formation, but is rather moving towards a model of managed and networked professionalism. The control of teacher training has gone from the university sector to government agencies. While it can be argued that the New Right (e.g. Conservative government 1979–1997) attacked teacher education they nonetheless retained a trust in teacher expertise and their capacity to decide how to teach. In contrast, New Labour polices, in the drive to raise standards, have increasingly asserted the state's role in deciding what and how to teach. Modernization of the workforce, competition and efficiency have both allowed and accelerated the growth of the new managerialism. Individual teachers are no longer key (or free) actors and their education has become a technically rational process of training, with a singular view of inculcating what constitutes good teaching to achieve successful results. Trainee teachers are measured against an ever-changing set of competencies which are to be 'got right' rather than challenged and debated (Furlong, 2005: 128). The continuing professional development of teachers is now closely controlled by government agencies and does not allow the aspiration of individual professional development but rewards short-term practical skills.

The impact of the dominant testing and assessment regime extends to pupils in two major ways; first, in terms of the changes in what pupils need to do in order to demonstrate effective learning and, secondly, in the social effects of increased emphasis on assessment and testing. James (2000), for example, suggests that the principal aims of the former Conservative governments were economic and instrumental, in ways that actively promoted competition in education. However, post-1997, with increased emphasis towards social inclusion, Prime Minister Blair argued for the development of both high levels of cognitive and interpersonal skills in education. The effect of adding the two has been to polarize levels of achievement (Tomlinson, 2003).

Pupils

The impact of these pressures on pupils is suggested in the title of two twenty-first-century articles: first, that pupils live 'measured lives' (James, 2000) and, secondly, that the curriculum is 'SATurated' (Hall et al., 2004). These measured lives are used as indices of the success of the system as well as monitoring the performance of teachers, schools and pupils. While this public agenda claims a general rise in standards, critics point out that closer examination of the detail indicates that these claims do not have genuine validity or, in fact, a solid reality (Tomlinson, 2003). For example, Brown et al. (2003) in a study of Year 4 pupils, challenge the notion that the national numeracy strategy is an overall success. They point out that the greatest improvement takes place for the mid-range students. The increase for high-achieving pupils is significantly less and there is also a decline in the achievement of low-attaining pupils, although the authors note an overall gain for boys as a whole. Wrigley (2006) also challenges the government's claim that maths achievement has risen, by noting evidence of a selective choice of baseline data. Drawing on work by Tymms et al. (2004), he criticizes the selective use of comparators, and suggests that the improvement in literacy is somewhat limited, if indeed it exists at all (Wrigley, 2006).

Class and achievement

Wrigley (2006) argues that rising scores are not necessarily indicative of real improvement, but they do offer the government the opportunity to claim success for the policy, as well as serving to divert attention from the increased divide in which the lower scores of working-class and ethnic minority children are not highlighted. In a similar vein, Cooper and Dunne (2000), in a study of pupil responses to items in mathematics, indicate that achievement can be strongly influenced by social class. They found that the use of con-textualized items for maths teaching placed working-class children in a disadvantaged position; that is, they were more likely to be confused by the setting, a situation in which they might fail to comprehend the purpose of the test. In a review of youth cohort data, Connolly (2006) identifies that the impact of class and ethnicity are greater than those of gender on GCSE attainment. Thus, girls are more likely to gain five or more GCSE grades A*–C than boys. Those from higher professional backgrounds are over eight times more likely to gain five or more higher grade GCSE passes, than those from 'routine' occupa-tional backgrounds. Those from lower professional backgrounds are a little over four times more likely to gain five, or more, higher GCSE passes. Chinese respondents were found to be about seven times more likely to gain five or more GCSE passes (ibid.). While govern-ment policy to break the link between poverty and class was restated in 2004, the 5-year strategy seems to be in contradiction with other education policies of diversity and choice, which reinforce class inequality (Harris and Ranson, 2005). Thus, for some pupils, the impact of testing and selection is to extend their relative disadvantage. This was noted by the former chief inspector for schools, who stated in 2003 that half of all 16-year-olds were not 'gaining' from the system (Tomlinson, 2003).

The decline of formative assessment

The overall decline in formative assessment has had a significant impact on the process and values of learning for pupils. Black et al. (2003) indicate that the use of assessment for learn-ing can be a constructive and interactive process between teachers and pupils. However, currently this form of assessment does not have a substantial role in the classroom, where preparation for Key Stage tests and external examinations have taken priority (Harlen, 2005). The effect of this is to make pupils more aware of performance than the process of learning and to increase anxiety, particularly in girls. This is exacerbated when the level of performance is exhibited publicly and used to compare other pupils and/or schools. This competitive pressure would appear to benefit boys in the classroom (Brown et al., 2003) and also encourage pupils to value performance and achievement over effort (Harlen, 2003).

Further evidence of the impact of the assessment regime on pupil learning can be found in a closer examination of the influence of whole class teaching. This emphasis means that pupils are less likely to be asked to provide elaborate responses to questions (Mroz et al., 2000) and more likely to be drilled in 'good' answers (Hall, 2004). James (2000) argues that the move to external testing has resulted in pupils engaging in shallow learning for factual tests. In turn, this produces a lack of motivation among pupils to do better, especially if they have already achieved an adequate standard, judged by the teacher against external criteria. In 2008, two of the major private schools withdrew from the league tables (for independ-ent schools) on the grounds that they were seen not to produce rounded pupils but instead turned them into 'exam junkies' (Lipsett, 2008).

Useful Websites

National Literacy Trust Section on formative assessment	www.literacytrust.org.uk/Database/assessment.html
Standards Site National Strategies – Secondary Education Official government website for secondary assessment	www.standards.dfes.gov.uk/secondary/framework/science/sgs/atspt/atspts
National Assessment Agency The National Assessment Agency (NAA) is responsible for the delivery of public exams and develops and delivers national curriculum assessments.	www.naa.org.uk/naa_15869.aspx
Stop the SATs An organisation of teachers and parents opposed to the current testing regime in schools	www.freewebs.com/nosats/

Pupils and tests

The social impact on pupils of the testing regime can be judged against the claim that it is providing a system which is inclusive of all pupils. For example, Hall (2004) describes how in classrooms, where assessment has become synonymous with SATs, children who are regarded as 'difficult' or 'challenging' tend to feel threatened by the tests. This not only encourages testing to be construed as another form of discipline by children who routinely challenge aspects of the classroom, but also has an adverse impact on quiet and less confident children. The pupil's sense of self is thus measured against their understanding relative to particular graded categories or classroom groups. These views are informed by the ways in which the teacher allocates access to booster classes, which can sometimes produce resentment in relation to additional help provided to those already able to achieve, but who are nevertheless coached to achieve the grade. In a review of the literature, on high-stakes testing, Harlen (2005) notes evidence that the introduction of the National Curriculum has led to a change in pupil motivation from intrinsic learning (for its own sake), to extrinsic learning for reward. Thus, pupils begin to rank themselves according to a teacher's perception of their potential within Key Stage tests. High-stakes testing, provides extrinsic reward for pupils but fails to provide intrinsic motivation for learning (Jones et al., 2003), thus undermining a long-term goal of lifelong learning and increasing the potential for pupils to view themselves as failures. As Wrigley (2006: 16) points out, 'boys are responding badly to one lesson in eight and the enquiry skills encouraged by subjects such as history, geography and technology are being neglected'. Hickey and Zuiker (2005) suggest that this is because policy makers do not engage with the issue of reduced intrinsic motivation or engagement when evaluating schools and teaching.

Activity

William (2003: 117) describes the McNamara Fallacy:

> The first step is to measure whatever can be easily measured. This is OK as far as it goes. The second step is to disregard that which can't easily be measured or to give it an arbitrary quantitative value. This is artificial and misleading, The third step is to presume that what can't be measured easily really isn't important. This is blindness. The fourth step is to say what can't be measured really doesn't exist. This is suicide.

He comments, that 'we start out with the aims of making the important measurable and ended up making only the measurable important'.

1. Is this a fair comment on the testing and standards regime?

Conclusion

In conclusion, it can be argued that all systems of testing and educational standards involve some notion of control, social reproduction and purpose to legitimate particular forms of knowledge. Since the introduction of the National Curriculum, the English school system has witnessed a regime of standards and testing which has become increasingly externally driven, regulated and high stake in operation. The results have been used not only to measure pupil achievement but also the performance of teachers, as well as the products of the system itself. This is stretching the boundaries of the technology of testing. The inferences drawn from such tests suggest progression along with increased knowledge, although outcomes indicating improved test scores are clearly not the same as any real increase in academic achievement. Evaluative statements, drawn from a range of summative test results, fail to reflect how single scores are achieved and do not take into account the background context of pupils and schools. The pressure, of a 'high-stakes' system, focuses the activities of pupils and teachers firmly on the goal of achieving appropriate test scores, and not necessarily on understanding some of the complexities of different forms of knowledge or even the goal of developing rounded personalities. This is reflected in the adoption of classroom pedagogy which elicits from pupils adequate sets of responses, rather than rewarding long-term learning goals. For pupils, this has emphasized the gap in performance and decreased the recognition of a range of achievements necessary for effective inclusion. The nature of teachers' professional competence has been constrained by the demands of an externally controlled and managed system. Both content and pedagogy are determined and success is imposed through performance. The impact of this regime has been to strengthen national control, emphasize hierarchy and elevate the value of performativity over developmental learning fostered by an empowered teaching profession.

Key Points

- There has been substantial growth in testing within the UK education system
- Testing is key to the selection of future elites in society
- Testing and assessment now represents a multimillion pound educational industry
- Testing is increasingly used as a mechanism to control teachers
- High-stakes tests are linked to external testing agencies
- Teacher-led formative assessment has declined in significance
- Testing has been identified as having a key role for the economy by the government
- The current testing regime does not take into account the impact that socio-economic conditions can have on pupil attainment
- There has been a decline in formative assessment that supports pupil learning
- Pupils are under increased pressure to perform, both by schools and parents
- Testing negatively impacts on issues relating to social inclusion and teacher perceptions of pupil needs.

Further Reading

Gipps, C. V. (1995) *Beyond Testing: Toward a Theory of Educational Assessment*, London: Falmer Press.

Warwick Mansell (2007) *Education by Numbers: The Tyranny of Testing*, London: Politicos.

Stephen Murdoch (2007) *IQ The Brilliant Idea That Failed*, London: Duckworth Overlook.

John White (2006) *Intelligence, Destiny and Education: The Ideological Roots of Intelligence Testing*, London: Routledge.

References

Abrams, L. M. and Madaus, G. F. (2003) 'The lessons of high stakes testing', *Education Leadership*, 61 (3): 31–5.

Alexander, R. (1997) *Policy and Practice in Primary Education*, London: Routledge.

Apple, M. (2004) *Ideology and the Curriculum* (3rd edition), London: Routledge.

Black, P. (1998a) *Testing Friend or Foe?* London: RoutledgeFalmer.

Black, P. (1998b) *Inside the Black Box: Raising Standards in the Classroom through Assessment*, London: NFER, Nelson.

Black, P., Harrison, C., Lee, C., Marshall, B. and William, G. (2003) *Assessment for Learning*, Maidenhead: Open University Press.

Broadfoot, P. (2000) 'Preface', in A. Filer (ed.), *Assessment Social Practice and Social Product*, London: RoutledgeFalmer.

Broadfoot, P. and Pollard, A. (2000) 'The changing discourse of assessment policy', in A. Filer (ed.), *Assessment Social Practice and Social Product*, London: RoutledgeFalmer.

Brown, M., Askew, M., Millet, A. and Rhodes, V. (2003) 'The key role of educational research in the development and evaluation of the National Numeracy Strategy', *British Education Research Journal*, 29 (5): 655–72.

Clarke, M., Madaus, G. and Horn, C. (2000) 'Retrospective on educational assessment and testing in the twentieth century', *Journal of Curriculum Studies*, 32 (2): 159–81.

Coffey, A. (2001) *Education and Social Change*, Buckingham: Open University Press.

Connolly, P. (2006) 'The effect of social class and ethnicity on gender differences in GCSE attainment', *British Educational Research Journal*, 32 (1): 3–21.

Cooper, B. and Dunne, M. (2000) 'Constructing the "legitimate" goal of a "realistic" maths item', in A. Filer (ed.), *Assessment Social Practice and Social Product*, London: RoutledgeFalmer.

Curtis, P. (2008) 'Pressure intensifies to cut school tests', *Guardian*, 10 May, http://education.guardian.co.uk/sats [accessed 10 May 2008].

Davis, A. (1998) *The Limits of Educational Assessment*, Oxford: Blackwell Publishers.

Docking, J. (2000) 'What is the problem?' in J. Docking (ed.), *New Labour's Policies for Schools*, London: David Fulton Publishers.

Elliott; J. and Hufton, N. (2000) 'International comparisons – what really matters?' in D. Shorrocks-Taylor and E. W. Jenkins (eds), *Learning from Others*, London: Kluwer Academic Publishers.

English, E., Hargraves, L. and Hislam, J. (2002) 'Pedagogical dilemmas in the national literacy strategy: primary teachers' perceptions, reflections and classroom behaviour', *Cambridge Journal of Education*, 32 (1): 9–26.

Filer, A. (2000) *Assessment Social Practice and Social Product*, London: RoutledgeFalmer.

Furlong, J. (2005) 'New Labour and teacher education: The end of an era', *Oxford Review of Education*, 31 (1): 119–34.

Gewirtz, S. (2000) 'Bringing the politics back in: a critical analysis of the quality discourse', *British Journal of Education Studies*, 48 (4): 352–79.

Gipps, C. V. (1995) *Beyond Testing: Toward a Theory of Educational Assessment*, London: Falmer Press.

Green, A. (1990) *Education and State Formation: The Rise of Education Systems in England, France and the USA*, London: Macmillan.

Hall, K. (2004) 'Schooling year 6, inclusion or SATuration?', in D. Hayes (ed.), *The Routledge Falmer Guide to Key Debates in Education*, London: RoutledgeFalmer, pp. 52–4.

Hall, K., Collins, J., Benjamin, S., Nind, M. and Sheehy, K. (2004) 'SATurated models of pupildom: assessment and inclusion/exclusion', *British Educational Research Journal*, 30 (6): 801–17.

Harlen, W. (2003) 'The inequitable impacts of high stakes testing', *Education Review*, 17 (1): 43–50.

Harlen, W. (2005) 'Trusting teacher judgement: Research evidence of reliability and validity of teacher's assessment used for summative purposes', *Research Papers in Education*, 20 (3): 245–270.

Harris, A. and Ranson, S. (2005) 'Contradictions of education policy', *British Education Research Journal*, 30 (5): 571–87.

Hickey, D. and Zuiker, S. (2005) 'Engaged participation: a sociocultural model of motivation with implications for educational assessment', *Educational Assessment*, 10 (3): 277–305.

James, M. (2000) 'Measured lives: the rise of assessment as the engine of change in English Schools', *Curriculum Journal*, 11 (3): 343–64.

Jones, G. M., Jones, B. D. and Hargrove, T. Y. (2003) *The Unintended Consequences of High Stakes Testing*, Oxford: Rowman and Littlefield Publishers.

Lipsett, A. (2008) 'Eton and St Paul's heads boycott independent schools' league tables', *Guardian*, 29 April, http://education.guardian.co.uk/publicschools/story [accessed 29 Apr. 2008].

Mroz, M., Smith, F. and Hardman, F. (2000) 'The discourse of the literacy hour', *Cambridge Journal of Education*, 30 (3): 379–90.

Pollard, A., Broadfoot, P., Croll, P., Osborn, M. and Abbott, D. (eds) (1994) *Changing English Primary Schools?: The Impact of the Education Reform Act at Key Stage 1*, London: Continuum.

Roscoe, N. (2000) 'A culture of testing is stifling investigation', *Biologist*, 54 (3): 125.

Shaw, D. (2000) 'Target setting, inspection and assessment', in J. Docking (ed.), *New Labour's Policies for Schools*, London: David Fulton.

Sheerman, B. (2008) quoted in P. Curtis (2008) 'Pressure intensifies to cut school tests', *Guardian*, 10 May, http://education.guardian.co.uk/sats [accessed 10 May 2008].

Sinnot, S. (2005) 'Government ignores KS2 assessment criticism', *Education*, 191: 2.

Smith, F., Hardman, F., Wall, K. and Mroz, M. (2004) 'Interactive whole class teaching in the National Numeracy and Literacy Strategies', *British Education Research Journal* 30 (3): 395–411.

Stewart, S. and Mansell, W. (2006) 'Coursework rethink targets GCSE Net', *Times Educational Supplement*, 4705: 10.

Tomlinson, M. (2003) quoted in J. Russell (2003) 'Tested to destruction, *Guardian*, 21 April, http://education.guardian.co.uk/schools [accessed 10 May 2008].

Tomlinson, S. (2006) 'New Labour and education', *Children and Society*, 17: 195–204.

Tymms, P., Merrell, C. and Jones, P. (2004) 'Using baseline assessment data to make international comparisons', *British Educational Research Journal*, 30 (5): 673–88.

William, D. (2000) 'The meaning and consequences of education assessment', *Critical Quarterly*, 42 (1): 105–27.

William, D. (2001) 'What's wrong with educational assessment', *Education Review* 15 (1): 57–62.

William, D. (2003) 'The meaning and consequences of education assessment', *Critical Quarterly*, 42 (1): 105–27.

Woodhead, C. (1998) quoted in D. Shaw (2000) 'Target setting, inspection and assessment', in J. Docking (ed.) *New Labour's Policies for Schools*, London: David Fulton.

Wrigley, T. (2006) *Another School is Possible*, London: Bookmark Publications.

Choice: Public, private and parents

Russell Jones and Elaine Mitchell

4

The UK context

Choice is a powerful concept. It carries associations of power, freedom and individual control that collectively, when placed in the context of childhood, assume a healthy state of being whereby institutions, parents and children have genuine opportunities to shape real decision-making in young peoples' lives. This chapter begins by challenging this notion and instead suggesting that there is a mythology of choice, and that the modern world for children is often populated with rhetoric and false choice rather than any real influence over important decisions that affect their lives.

It is not difficult to trace back the significant political notions of choice for parents. In the early 1980s, schools began a transitional process that brought them into line with a political philosophy based on market forces. Very broadly, it was believed that a healthy economy and the well-being of its people relied on a system whereby the market would be given free rein and determine the way in which services and goods were made available to people. Many argued that this was perhaps appropriate as a system in which healthy notions of competition kept prices in check and encouraged a climate whereby high-quality goods and services at the right price would thrive (and conversely, poor quality goods and services that are overpriced would fail). Many also argued however, that while this may sometimes be a productive philosophy, this was more often a less than productive way to conceive of education and children's services.

To place the education system in a competitive market meant that there would be fundamental change to the whole process of education and this was 'sold' to the electorate as freedom of choice: freedom to choose a successful school over a failing school, freedom to choose a school with particular conventions, beliefs and faiths, and freedom to challenge the assumed authority of the school. In this climate, schools became no different to any other market provider and instead of working on collaborative projects for the benefit of pupils, they found themselves allocating school funds to enter into competition with their neighbours.

Kentucky Fried Schooling

In case there is doubt about the legitimacy of this analogy, it is worth revisiting the kind of writing at that time that supported these notions. One writer referred to the New Right's conception of education as Kentucky Fried Schooling, where schools are run as businesses with the parent as the customer and the pupil as the product (Epstein, 1993: 24). Again, this is not as ludicrous as might be imagined when statements from this period are closely examined. For example, one MP suggested that schools should aspire to the standards of Marks & Spencers in 'guaranteeing a choice of quality goods served by well trained staff in a disciplined environment under the supervision of strong management' (Jones, 1989: 51). Similarly, right-wing educationalists were able to sum up their philosophies with statements such as 'Equality in education is as daft as equality in supermarkets. There is no such thing and there is never going to be' (O'Keeffe, 1990: 59).

Market forces

The idea that market forces could determine quality in schools and children's services in exactly the same way as quality is determined in a supermarket is part of the mythology proposed here. Many parents clearly did not have choice at all. For some, there was one school and one choice. For others the choice meant transporting pupils to schools out of the catchment area (assuming that the pupil was given a place to begin with) and this incurred further cost, disruption to friendship groups, alienation to communities and families and it is not too difficult to see that while some parents in particular settings with particular resources at their disposal had choices to make, the same choices for most parents were part of the myth.

Similarly, the support for notions of choice didn't come from pupils, parents or professions; it was political. The voices of professionals had been all but eradicated with the abolition of the Schools Council; the changing composition of governing bodies gave more voices to local businessmen and businesswomen and of course children's voices were, as ever, absent from the debate. Choice became something that was sold to the electorate as politically and personally desirable when in fact it only ever really existed for a select few.

National Curriculum

The introduction of the National Curriculum can, then, be seen as part of this process. If the provider is to demonstrate the quality of the goods, then a mechanism needs to be devised whereby those goods can be compared, measured and contrasted to allow the customer free choice [*sic*]. In order to further assure high quality, a team of product inspectors then need to be given the authority to make quality assured judgements about the quality of the services on offer. Remembering that prior to Ofsted, schools could count on a network of local education advisers (who could come into school and provide professional support and advice to enhance practice), then the shift to inspection was very revealing. Along with the legal status of an imposed curriculum and the new inspectorate came the language of compliance. This was significant in that providers of education for children who did not comply with the government's view on what counted as high-quality education were then non-compliant, and liable to be taken over by super-heads or closed down. In terms of choice it is again worth noting that notions of compliance were not established by parents (who were told it was they who had the choice) or by children (who still had no voice or choice); this was raw political will being sold as parental power.

As pointed out elsewhere, parental choice of school has, effectively, been limited since the 1988 Education Reform Act (ERA) that purported to create new parental rights. It has been claimed that the ERA:

> embodies a highly regulated version of school choice, which allows parents to choose among government-run schools all of which are constrained by a detailed national curriculum, and which also gives schools the power to select among applicants. (Brighouse, 2000: 19)

The author goes on to indicate a very different shift in, for example, New Zealand, Australia and some states of the US at the same time as the ERA which set out to work more productively with disadvantaged children and families. These initiatives took the form of a much more radical agenda of social justice that challenged superficial notions of choice in favour of making schools more responsible for encouraging wider participation and building more appropriate curricula.

Stop, Read and Reflect

Research findings: School admissions

A National Foundation for Educational Research (NFER) study found that:

- Voluntary aided primary and secondary schools admitted lower numbers of children eligible for free school meals, compared to their proportion in the communities the schools served

⇨

Stop, Read and Reflect—cont'd

- Pupils of Black Ethnic Minority (BEM) origin travelled outside their local communities more than white pupils
- Voluntary aided secondary schools admitted lower numbers of SEN pupils in proportion to their numbers in the local communities. (Chamberlain et al., 2006)

A Sutton Trust survey found that:

- In 2007, three-quarters of the schools in the top 200 (*highest performing comprehensive schools*) were responsible for their own admissions, compared with just over half in 1998. These schools tend to be more socially exclusive, *pupils on free school meals compared with 8.1% in local authority controlled schools*...(The Sutton Trust, 2008)

Research and Information on State Education found that:

- In a significant minority of schools, notably those that are their own admissions authorities – voluntary-aided and foundation schools – a variety of criteria are used which appear to be designed to select groups of pupils and exclude others. These include children of employees; children of former pupils; partial selection by ability/aptitude in a subject area or by general ability; and children with a family connection to the school. (West and Hind, 2003)

Question

1. Taking this research into account, what impact do you think these findings have on the ability of parents and pupils to choose their school?

The reality of choice

Britain in the twenty-first century has become something of a battleground when it comes to notions of parental, children and community rights in relation to school. Notions of choice, for example, are difficult to maintain when more than 26,000 thousand families appealed against the decision by local authorities to send children to schools against the wishes of the parents (a figure that is 205 greater than the previous year) (Cassidy, 2008). It is worth acknowledging that the vast majority of appeals are related to placement in early years and primary settings, which may indicate that parents are aware of the significance of their allocated places and are clearly arguing for real choice.

> Critics said the figures showed parents were increasingly frustrated at the poor quality of local schools. But ministers insisted families had more choice thanks to the 'massive increase' in the number of good schools in England since Labour came to power. (Cassidy, 2008)

Of course there are socio-metric, geographical and economic dimensions to this case; numerous organizations (again including the Children's Society) have outlined class-related divisions in school access meaning that children from poorer areas of the country have fewer real 'choices' and are often placed in poor schools. This evidence is an indication that parents, children and communities do want choice and have to enter appeal procedures to access and demonstrate that choice. Whether the choices they seek are real choices or not is another matter for discussion – for example, how much real choice can there be when curriculum content and delivery alongside the training of teachers are centrally controlled and policed? Perhaps, at this stage, we should be starting to question whether New Labour's policies really are about creating a truly inclusive environment for children and genuinely tackling issues such as social exclusion, or whether these are unachievable goals while swept in the tide of market forces and consumerism? They certainly appear to demonstrate a contradictory approach while espousing a war on child poverty and simultaneously promoting 'inclusion', they are not only allowing but promoting market forces in the control, capitalization and commodification of education.

Secondary education

The situation in the secondary sector is equally problematic, and it has been reported that over one hundred thousand parents failed to get their children into their first-choice secondary school in 2007. In addition:

> A total of 3,126 parents in England were not made a single offer of a school place. 'These figures show that for large numbers of parents the idea they can choose a school for their children is a myth', said Michael Gove, the Conservatives' schools spokesman. (Garner, 2008)

The situation in secondary schools is made more problematic as a new admissions code came into force in 2007 which meant that schools are no longer allowed to interview parents and now have the right to hold lotteries to resolve admissions procedures. This code's intention was to deliberately address contemporary social divisions and undermine reports that wealthier, middle-class parents had learned how to manipulate the admissions systems and were able to create choice for themselves and their children. Several reports (most notably the Good Childhood Inquiry – see Children's Society, 2007a, 2007b) have outlined the extent to which parents are prepared to go to secure their notion of choice and the popular picture created is one of a body of parents who are ready to lie, cheat and even move home to achieve these ends:

> More than half of parents are prepared to move home or lie about where they live in order to provide their children with a good education, a survey has found. Research for the Children's Society also confirmed that some parents – one in seven – are willing to pose as practising church-goers, to gain access to a better school. In London – where the battle for good placements is at its most competitive – the proportion of those who admitted to being dishonest rose to 23 per cent. The report portrayed a strong class divide in school access, with poor children being stuck living in areas with worse schools. (Macintyre, 2007)

Clearly, the likelihood is that the code will result in further appeals and this adds fuel to the notion of 'disgruntled' parents who are unhappy with their lack of choice in educational matters. That said, there remains considerable tension in the field of educational 'choice':

> In fairness, the Government recognises this, which is why it is establishing more independent academies and foundation schools and also attempting to give parents more 'choice' over their children's education as a means of driving up standards. Legitimate questions can be asked over whether ministers are moving fast enough. But at least they recognise that reform is necessary. This is more than can be said for the teaching unions, which have become the main obstacles to the establishment of more academies and remain stubbornly hostile to attempts to cater for the rising expectations of parents regarding their children's education. (Independent, 2008)

Every Child Matters

The question needs to be asked: if all children fall under the remit of Every Child Matters (ECM) (DfES, 2004) and if every child does indeed matter then should not educational provision be of the highest and uniform standard despite a postcode? Increasingly, it seems as though choice in education appears to be only for parents who can afford it and who can 'choose' to live in areas where the 'best' schools are situated while others are often restricted to only a bargain basement of educational provision. Research supported by the Joseph Rowntree Foundation states that there are good schools which are 'particularly effective in helping students to avoid low achievement', however they 'are not uniformly distributed across local authorities and they are concentrated in some local authorities more than others' (Cassen and Kingdon, 2007: 11). According to Stephen Ball of London University's Institute of Education, class inequalities are as prominent now as ever before. He argues this typifies an apartheid system of schooling that sees a return to a tiered approach where working, middle and upper class reserve social class boundaries through financial affordability (Curtis, 2008). It is questionable and certainly concerning that Britain still seems to be maintaining and perpetuating an educational under-class, driven by the education system and hidden under the guise of choice.

Activity

Research the evidence relating to the way choice operates for different communities and make notes on either of the following questions:

1. How can Britain begin to offer real choice to a culturally diverse population of parents and pupils?
2. In what ways can policy makers and institutional gatekeepers begin to be more responsive to the diverse needs of twenty-first-century Britain.

European comparisons

At the present time, it is worth mentioning the various European and Scandinavian models (to which we are told the UK regularly aspires) as a means of comparison. In Finland, there is a co-operative model of school leadership, which means that often, Heads are nominated for the role by colleagues on the school's staff and only serve a fixed term before the role is handed on. Major leadership roles within the school are often shared to take account of personal and professional expertise and this is seen as a direct attempt to remain responsive to the needs of parents and local communities. The Finnish education system has moved from a centrally controlled model (where the National Curriculum measured over seven hundred pages in the mid-1970s) to a decentralized model that is based around aspirations of equity and social justice. Parents are not allowed to 'opt-out' of the system (there are no private, fee-paying schools) and the intention is to create an educational climate where the 'freedom to innovate' is of paramount importance. From personal experience, we witnessed this first hand in one Finnish school where a highly regarded and highly qualified teacher went on a 6-month secondment to America but, by personal choice, still gave three or four electronic lessons a week to her school's population. Teaching is a highly respected and valued profession in Finland; for example, Finland's top 10 per cent of graduates go into teaching in contrast to the bottom third in the US, which regularly performs poorly in international tests (Hepburn, 2008).

Sweden

In Sweden, parental choice was a virtually meaningless concept until 1994, as up until this point in time there was no choice in the state system. From this date however, legislation and reform made it much easier for funding to be directed to newly created independent schools that reflected the aspirations and philosophies of parents, children and communities. The system in Sweden, for example, offers parents more radical and realistic choices meaning that they can send their children through 'conventional' schools or instead choose for Friskola or Fridaskolen (or 'Freedom School') system where the curriculum, the power relationships and children's participation and negotiation are all part of a realistic system of real choice. Gunnar Hökmark, an MEP for the Swedish Moderate Party suggests that:

> The free-school reform provides parents and children with a choice suitable for their specific needs. Tax money set aside for education is divided per child and can be used for any school following the national curriculum and approved by the authorities, whether it is a state school or a free school. There are now about 900 free schools in Sweden, which have become an excellent option for parents, and teachers, who are not satisfied with state education. In addition, all research shows that where there are free schools, the state schools perform better. (Hökmark, 2008)

This move has been supported by the range of political parties and has meant that choice has become a reality for around eighty-three thousand children (or 8 per cent of the school population):

> These new independent schools are not only providing a high quality of education, but there is also strong evidence to suggest the competition they provide is having a beneficial effect on municipal

schools in driving up standards. Not surprisingly, 90 per cent of parents support the principle. (Monteith, 2005)

The Netherlands

In the Netherlands the differences in funding systems and parental choice is pronounced. Children are allocated 'price tags' which means that schools receive a certain amount of funding for each child. 'Price tags' are accorded to socio-economic background rather than 'one-size-fits-all'; a particularly important measure given the high numbers of migrant and non-Dutch-speaking pupils who are part of their education system. This is also seen as centrally important as it confirms the notion that parental choice in education is an accepted part of the Dutch constitution. On this basis, independent schools flourish, meaning that many different kinds of schools are in operation, many different approaches to the curriculum exist and parents have real choice about what they want for their children. Currently, 70 per cent of Dutch children attend some form of 'independent' school and parents and pupil numbers are the defining feature behind the success of each institution:

> Not being constrained by catchment areas also gives parents more choice – in the Netherlands it seems to work along the lines of, 'if I can get there by bike it's an option'. But what it really means is that parents don't snare themselves in mortgages to get into catchment areas they can't afford, or pay expensive school fees or face the humiliation of having to rediscover a lapsed faith. They can choose whichever school will suit their child best. Not all parents make an active choice but enough do to influence the standard of schools everywhere. (Schreiber, 2008)

Comparing models

In the context of this chapter, it is important to recognize that these models are not simply transferable or adaptable to the needs of British children, parents and communities. Indeed, to some extent, this has been the failing of the present policy makers who have seen opportunities to 'lift' interesting or socially 'worthy' elements of these educational models. It does not work. These models are built on philosophical and egalitarian principles that inform policy making. All participants (including children!) are valued and their views are seen as valuable contributions to the whole. Reijo Laukkanen, a member of the Finnish Board of Education explains: 'What's very important in my mind is you must take the context, history and other factors in your society seriously and build on them.... You can't change an education system and guidelines every year...if you have consensus though, you can really make efforts to get to the dreams you have' (Hepburn, 2008). Perhaps it is worth considering notions of consensus in Britain more fully to understand the ways in which parental and pupil choice operate differently here. While disgruntled parents are left to argue their personal corners and centralized government makes sweeping legislative decisions about educational policy (and while children have largely been absent from the whole process) it is hardly surprising that we have a lack of educational consensus or vision to guide future policy.

Again, from personal experience, we were witness to the building of a new Finnish primary school in the north of the country where the prospective pupils had been surveyed at the design stage, meaning that the finished glass and steel construction was a direct response to children's request for few dark corridors and 'as much light as possible'. Parents and educationalists had been surveyed about its location and it was built next door to the local university so that both sets of professionals could benefit from each others' expertise. Compare this with recent reports that despite pledges from central government that reforms would support parents' ability to choose schools, it is claimed that the current system is so inflexible that this is wholly unrealistic, if not entirely impossible. It is claimed that parents are forced to compete with each other for school places because of the nature of the educational market, and that:

> In a system of inflexible supply, parent demand is not harnessed as a force to drive up standards – instead, securing places at the best performing school is a zero sum game, and one which better-off parents tend to 'win' at the expense of the less well-off…in other words, if schools do not have to compete with one another, then parents are forced to. (Lipsett, 2008)

Activity

Use the evidence and arguments presented in this chapter to create a poster that answers the following question:

1. Is there something so different about Britain that we no longer have the ability to create institutional support for our young people that all participants and stakeholders see as valuable?

The future of 'choice' in the UK

While New Labour have been (understandably) keen to highlight evidence of improvement in educational attainment, it is increasingly obvious that there remains significant numbers of pupils who have slipped through the net of our education system. The postcode lottery whereby pupils continue to access and receive educational provision differently continues to be a particular problem for policy makers, parents and pupils alike. A recent report by the Bow Group, a Centre-right think tank, pointed out that since the party came to power, almost a million young people have left school without having achieved five GCSEs at grade G (the lowest grade possible). The Report also found that '3.9 million pupils, close to sixty per cent of the total, who had not gained five C grades at GCSE, including in the core subjects of English and maths' (Asthana, 2008). In a recent examination of the way in which these outcomes are shaped by the postcode lottery for school places, it was argued that, for example, parents who live in Hammersmith and Fulham, Westminster or North Somerset stand a less than 3 per cent chance of winning a school place on appeal, whereas parents who live in North Lincolnshire, Durham and Rotherham are more than 75 per cent likely to win places for their children on appeal (Curtis, 2008).

Parental concerns

Parents are only too aware of the value and significance of education and increasingly they have come to recognize relative powerlessness in the selection and admissions procedures based on geographical and socio-economic factors that leave them frustrated at the clear lack of equity or real opportunity. Among others, Scott (2006) highlights the stark differences between higher socio-economic groups and attainment and those from poorer communities and poorer schools. He asserts 'inequalities of life chances in education . . . are especially important, as these are central to the reproduction of class relations' (Scott, 2006: 46). These life chances according to Payne (2006) refer to the chances a person has during their lifetime, such as income, education, health, employment, etc. and these chances are intrinsically linked to social class. While ministers are approving a new admissions code to tackle this kind of problem, it is increasingly self-evident that Britain still maintains and perpetuates an educational underclass; children from poorer families are worst hit as disadvantaged areas are likely to have fewer highly rated schools and so only wealthier parents have any real power over the choice and quality of their children's education.

Stop, Read and Reflect

In 2007 Brighton and Hove Local Education Authority announced a change to the school admissions system for secondary education. The proposal put forward by the authority was that admission to oversubscribed schools would be based on a random lottery of applicants. The process excluded sibling links and home–school distance. The lottery system would allow all potential pupils to an oversubscribed school an equal chance to obtain a place.

However, middle-class parents objected to this proposal and took the local authority to court. The courts ruled against the parents and the new system is being implemented for the new intake of pupils in September 2008.

The opposition to the lottery became a very political issue with the Conservative Party backing the parental opposition to the lottery system. The battle is clearly over educational resources and control of a perceived advantage that parents feel some schools have over others. It also signals the fact that middle-class parents have been able in the past to manipulate the schools' admissions system through the housing market and their ability to purchase property.

Although the lottery is not ideal, it is the fairest way of distributing perceived scarce resources. The ideal solution would be for all local schools to be a good school that any parent would be happy to send their child.

⇨

For more information on this story any of the major broadsheet newspapers or the BBC will have relevant reports.

The Guardian   www.guardian.co.uk/
The Times   www.timesonline.co.uk/tol/news/

It should be noted different newspapers will take a different perspective due to their political position.

Question

1. Do you think that a lottery system is the fairest method of allocating school places? Explain and provide evidence for your answer.

In the midst of the struggle for control of both the values and resources of the education system, arguably the least consulted participants are children themselves. While policy makers have focused on performance indicators, inspection and league tables, the notion that children's role as participants in this process has been all but systematically ignored. Who thought to ask what a child wants from their educational experience? Schools Councils have clearly been a cosmetic exercise in democracy in some institutions and even when they have been encouraged and supported, the voices and concerns of children have had little impact on real issues of choice in the curriculum or over teaching and learning policies.

The Universal Declaration of Human Rights

The Universal Declaration of Human Rights (UDHR) specified in 1948 that 'Parents have a prior right to choose the kind of education that shall be given to their children.' In twenty-first-century Britain it seems that children are still merely commodities rather than consumers in the educational market place despite being the subject of the United Nations Convention on the Rights of the Child (UNCRC), and the Children Act 1989, 2004 which argues that children do have, after all, the entitlement to be listened to. Indeed the UNCRC not only 'affirms the difference of children' but specifically 'gives rights to children only and insofar as they are children'. It is questionable whether as parents and society as a whole we merely pay lip service to giving children real agency in their lives and particularly in an educational context. Even if parents have choice, it is seldom passed onto children and this happens even less frequently in schools.

Conclusion

Having argued that there is a continued mythology around notions of choice, and that of all stakeholders and participants it is children themselves who have been powerless and silent in this debate, it is worth pointing towards the future and looking at the ways in which this may change. The key legislative change is the ten-year, 1 billion pounds Children's Plan due to commence in September 2008. When looking at 'choice' and 'power' it has been argued that decision-making has been politically expedient rather than a characteristic modern democratic Britain, and that other countries have had a radically different starting point when thinking about children, parents, education and services. Perhaps the Children's Plan is the first demonstrative attempt to genuinely address this issue and realign British notions of choice.

There is no doubting that this initiative rose out of the damning study published by the Children's Society that resulted in headlines such as: 'Britain's Children are the Unhappiest in the Western World' (Blair, 2007) and 'UK Children the Unhappiest in Europe' (Carrell, 2006). The study, undertaken by academics at the University of York, looked at children's material wealth, housing, safety, education, well-being and relationships across all 25 member states of the EU in order to produce a league table of child well-being. It placed the UK 21st in the table ahead only of Latvia, Estonia, Lithuania and Slovakia. Cynics would say that visible political change was needed to address this situation but clearly the drive behind the Children's Plan has been to place children themselves at the heart of change. While the Plan is broad and comprehensive in its attempts to address several areas of children's lives it is clear that disadvantage and social justice are key concerns in its design. As well as commitments to improve facilities for play and to initiate positive activities for young people in sport, drama and art, there are commitments to address a root and branch review of assessment and the primary curriculum, to address the issue of overtesting and create much stronger and more informative and supportive links between parents and educational institutions, particularly in areas of social deprivation and where children experience poverty in their lives.

The issue then, is to consider whether the mythology of choice is still present in the lives of stakeholders and participants. Is the Children's Plan an indication of a clear political, social and economic commitment to changing children's lives for the better, and to create a climate where parental choice and the child's voice has real meaning and currency? Alternatively, is this another example of policy developed 'on the hoof' in a crisis response to unfavourable media reports, and another set of uncoordinated initiatives leaving the root causes of poverty, deprivation and injustice untouched? The Shadow Children's Secretary dismissed the Children's Plan as a:

> Missed opportunity (which was) an underwhelming collage with items stuck on any old how and no underlying vision…instead of a broad and deep vision we have a disappointingly hesitant and patchy programme, which betrays an itch to intervene but no grasp of the real problems. (Gove, 2007)

Critically, it could be argued that genuine choice, parental involvement and children's welfare are not determined by political initiatives; instead they are the daily concerns of the stakeholders; the collective interests of the participants and the ability of institutions such as schools to respond to and meet the aspirations of its clients. When these concerns, interests and aspirations are heard collectively (and subsequent decision-making and policy follows appropriately) it could be argued that the result is happier children, more involved parents and more responsive institutions. Where political will attempts to shape and determine choice, where it systematically ignores the voices, concerns and interests of children, parents and other participants, and where it realigns institutional priorities to place demonstrated and measured performance over the needs of pupils and parents, then the result is likely to produce disharmony, resentment, frustration and stasis.

Key Points

- Choice is a powerful and appealing concept that seems to empower individuals
- The notion of choice became a political issue from the 1980s onwards as this is the start of the development of market-driven social policies
- As part of these market-driven policies it was envisioned that schools would become and act like small businesses, for example, Kentucky Fried Schooling
- The introduction of the National Curriculum and the associated reforms are all key to creating a market in education
- Education is still faced by issues of social inequality that impact disproportionately for poor children and families
- New Labour's commitment to creating an inclusive education system might now be questioned
- The problem of social segregation is greater in secondary education
- The UK does not compare favourably with European countries such as Finland or Sweden
- Parents feel increasingly powerless in the school selection and admissions process
- Education has an impact on an individual's life chances
- Choice is a myth in education
- Genuine choice is about the ability of schools and communities to respond to the aspirations of all those involved in them, rather than through political initiatives and political rhetoric.

Further Reading

Cassen, R. and Kingdon, G. (2007) *Tackling Low Educational Achievement*, York: Joseph Rowntree Foundation.

David Gillborn (2008) *Racism and Education Coincidence or Conspiracy*, London: Routledge.

Mark Olsen, John Codd and Anne-Marie O'Neill (2004) *Education Policy Globalization, Citizenship and Democracy*, London: Sage.

Sally Tomlison (2005) (2nd edition) *Education in a Post-Welfare Society*, Maidenhead: Open University Press.

References

Asthana, A. (2008) 'One million pupils failed by Labour exam policy', *The Observer*, 20 April 2008, http://education.guardian.co.uk/gcses/story/0,,2275280,00.html [accessed 3 July 2008].

Blair, A. (2007) 'Britain's children are the unhappiest in the Western world', *The Times*, 14 February 2007, www.times-online.co.uk/tol/news/uk/health/article1381571.ece [accessed 4 July 2008].

Brighouse, H. (2000) *School Choice and Social Justice*, Oxford: Oxford University Press.

Carrell, S. (2006) 'British children the unhappiest in Europe says study', *The Independent*, 10 September 2006, www.independent.co.uk/news/uk/this-britain/uk-children-the-unhappiest-in-europe-says-study-415387.html [accessed 2 July 2008].

Cassen, R. and Kingdon, G. (2007) *Tackling Low Educational Achievement*, York: Joseph Rowntree Foundation.

Cassidy, S. (2008) 'Number of primary school appeals up by 20%', *The Independent*, 23 May 2008, www.independent.co.uk/news/education/education-news/number-of-primary-school-appeals-up-by-20-per-cent-832853.html [accessed 6 July 2008].

Chamberlain, T., Rutt, S. and Fletcher-Campbell, F. (2006) *Admissions: Who Goes Where? Messages from the Statistics*, Slough: NFER.

Children's Society (2007a) *The Good Childhood Inquiry*, www.childrenssociety.org.uk [accessed 1 July 2008].

Children's Society (2007b) *Reflections on Childhood – Learning*, www.childrenssociety.org.uk/resources/documents/good%20childhood/Reflections%20on%20Childhood%20Learning_3193_full.pdf [accessed 1 July 2008].

Curtis, P. (2008) 'Parents face postcode lottery over school place appeals', *Guardian*, 23 May, www.education.guardian.co.uk/admissions/story/0,,2281768,00.html [accessed 5 July 2008].

Department for Education and Skills (2004) *Every Child Matters – Change for Children*, London: DfES.

Epstein, D. (1993) *Changing Classroom Cultures: Anti-racism, Politics and Schools*, Stoke-on-Trent: Trentham Books.

Garner, R. (2008) 'Parents failed on school choice, say Tories', *The Independent*, 26 February 2008, www.independent.co.uk/news/education/education-news/parents-failed-on-school-choice-say-tories-787275.html [accessed 8 July 2008].

Gove, M. (2007) 'Play and learning children's plan', BBC News, 11 December, http://news.bbc.co.uk/1/hi/education/7136564.stm [accessed 4 July 2008].

Hepburn, H. (2008) 'We place trust in our teacher', *The Times Educational Supplement*, 21 March 2008, www.tes.co.uk/search/story/?story_id=2596476 [accessed 5 July 2008].

Hökmark, G. (2008) 'Sweden's recent reforms have been hugely successful', *Guardian*, 17 April, www.guardian.co.uk/commentisfree/2008/apr/17/davidcameron.conservatives [accessed 6 July 2008].

Independent (2008) 'The myth of choice and parental power in our schools' (unauthored Lead Article), *The Independent*, 4 March 2008, www.independent.co.uk/opinion/leading-articles/leading-article-the-myths-of-choice-and-parental-power-in-our-schools-in-schools-790890.html [accessed 4 July 2008].

Jones, K. (1989) *Right Turn: The Conservative Revolution in Education*, London: Hutchinson Radius.

Lipsett, A. (2008) 'School choice still restricted', *Guardian*, 10 June, www.education.guardian.co.uk/schoolfunding/story/0,,2284727,00.html [accessed 1 July 2008].

Macintyre, J. (2007) 'Parents lie to secure best school for children', *The Independent*, 17 October 2007, www.independent.co.uk/news/education/education-news/parents-lie-to-secure-best-school-for-children-397082.html [accessed 2 July 2008].

Monteith, B. (2005) 'Sweden's path to real parent choice', *Times Educational Supplement*, 18 February 2005, www.tes.co.uk/search/story/?story_id=2074658 [accessed 10 July 2008].

O'Keeffe, D. (1990) *The Wayward Elite*, London: Adam Smith Institute.

Payne, G. (ed.) (2006) *Social Divisions*, Hampshire: Palgrave Macmillan.

Schreiber, N. (2008) 'Why can't the English be more like the Dutch?' *The Independent*, 22 May 2008, www.independ-ent.co.uk/news/education/schools/nikki-schreiber-why-cant-the-english-be-more-like-the-dutch-831862.html [accessed 7 July 2008].

Scott, J. (2006) 'Class and stratification', in G. Payne (ed.) *Social Divisions* Hampshire: Palgrave Macmillan.

The Sutton Trust (2008) *Low Income Pupils in High Performing Comprehensive Schools*. Available at: www.suttontrust.com/reports/BallotsInSchoolAdmissions.pdf [accessed 24 Sept. 2008].

West, A. and Hind, A. (2003) *Secondary School Admissions in England: Exploring the Extent of Overt and Covert Selection*, Rise: London School of Economics.

Part Two
Marginalization and Education

Faith schools: Diversity or division?

Derek Kassem and Lisa Murphy

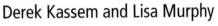

Chapter Outline

Introduction

This chapter sets out to examine, in the context of the British education system, the increasing prominence of faith schools – schools with a direct religious focus. The current government, and all the major political parties within the UK, are committed to faith-based schools and/or their expansion. This is particularly true within the secondary phase, which caters for 11- to 18-year-olds. The expansion of faith-based institutions and their wider role in the education system, as a whole, is however not without some notable controversy. It is important that the reader recognizes the extent to which faith-based institutions impact on the education system. Faith institutions exist at all levels of the school system, ranging from those that serve the youngest children to those that educate 18-year-olds. However, church organizations also run former teacher-training institutions that now have university status. The extent of religious influence on the education system is not limited to the direct education of children and control of the process of teacher training. There is also a legal requirement that every school carries out a daily act of worship, which is broadly Christian in ethos and form. Coupled with this is the legal requirement that religious education within schools must again be broadly Christian in nature and purpose. The overpowering influence of religious organizations within the state education system is witnessed by a report in the *Observer* newspaper (Asthana, 2007). This recounted the efforts of a headteacher (in charge of one of the government's new flagship Trust schools), being told by senior government officials that it was a 'political impossibility' for him to run his school along broadly secular lines. This, of course, raises questions as to the nature and purpose of education that young people receive, along with the ability of schools to deal with an increasingly diverse society.

The social context of faith schools

Against the background of the increasing secularization and changing nature of British society, this chapter seeks to examine the contemporary issue of faith-based schools, and further analyse the impact of their recent expansion within the education system. Current trends towards wider difference and diversity in terms of culture, ethnicity and religious beliefs are having a major impact on perceived levels of social cohesion within the UK. It can thus be argued that faith schools will act as a divisive impediment to the future structure and well-being of British society. Accordingly, in the process of examining the role of faith schools, including the impact of their expansion within the secondary phase of education, this chapter will consider a number of critical issues: the impact of Islamophobia on education; the decline of churchgoing population in the UK; social and ethnic segregation within our school system and the rights of the child to receive an education that will allow them to develop into independent, autonomous adults. It should be noted that this chapter is deliberately not written from the perspective of a balanced account of these issues. Rather, it adopts a standpoint that education should be secular in nature and that the teaching of religious faith, no matter what form, should not be promoted or subsidized by the state. Instead, faith should be a matter of individual conscience.

Types of faith schools

Within the UK, there are a number of different types of school. This has been the case for a considerable period of time but with the context of present policy, of the diversification of education provision, the number of types of school provided by the state has increased. The main faith-based schools fall into two categories: volunteer controlled schools and voluntary aided schools. For the former, the responsibility for running the school is jointly held by the local authority and the church to which the school is affiliated. However, for these schools the local authority is usually the dominant partner and is responsible for all aspects of admission and most of the funding. For voluntary aided faith schools, however, the balance of power is more equally shared between the faith organization and the local authority, in that there are more governors from the faith group that play a role in controlling admissions and staffing. Even so, the majority of funding is still provided by the state. Government policy has over the past ten years also introduced another type of school that is outside the control of local authorities, but still funded by the state; these are the Academies. Academies are part of the Government's clear-cut policy of providing greater diversity within state education. Of the 100 Academies so far started by the government, 42 of them are sponsored by faith-based organizations (Odone, 2008). It should also be noted that some of these faith-based organizations are in many respects controversial in that they are not mainstream Christian organizations, but rather led by fundamentalists committed to ideas such as creationism and intelligent design, which they seek to have taught in the schools they control (Harris, 2005). The influence of these organizations on education goes beyond the area of religious belief and into the realm of science education. This is clearly a matter of some concern and yet it only raises limited debate among politicians, educationalists, parents and academics. This entrenched fundamentalism within some of these recently created schools is certainly not new. During the nineteenth century, in various parts of the country, dissenting Christians held sway of the education system – a point that is especially true of Wales. The issue here is that there seems to be something of an abandonment of the state defined curriculum, the national curriculum, to the influence of particular religious groups.

The justification of faith-based schools

There are many and various justifications of faith-based schools. McGettrick (2005) argues that in promoting spirituality these schools counter those elements of government policy, which adopt a utilitarian view of education that emphasizes the needs of the economy. A further point of justification is suggested in the work of Jackson (2003) and Cush (2003), who separately adopt a similar approach in attempting to justify faith schools in terms of equal opportunities, or otherwise as a positive response to racism for ethnic minority pupils. However, Cush (2005) also claims that faith schools provide for a tolerant and life-enhancing community, with high academic achievement for their pupils. Cush (ibid.) also suggests that faith-based schools provide for an intercultural environment that promotes social inclusion. Interestingly, this argument is also to be found in government publications which claim:

> The Government and faith school providers believe that **all** (DCSF emphasis) – whether they have a religious character or not play a key role in providing a safe and harmonious environment. . . . The faith school providers who sponsor schools with a religious character often also have a particular

role in helping to meet the needs of those people in their faith communities who would otherwise be hard to reach, thus enabling them to integrate into society. (DCSF, 2007: 1)

The range of justifications for faith schools given above, as well as those mentioned elsewhere (see, for example, Brighouse, 2005; Parker-Jenkins et al., 2005; Odone, 2008), seem to rest on two major arguments. First, it is suggested that such schools can reach minority groups in society and provide a more inclusive and meritocratic environment. Second, and most importantly, the argument frequently comes down to the idea that faith-based schools provide a better education for their pupils than their supposedly non-faith-based counterparts. This contention is a fiercely debated one and also one of questionable validity. Before discussing this claim in detail, it is necessary to examine the context in which the government is pursuing its faith school agenda.

Faith schools and health programmes

Vaccination against cervical cancer

It was reported in the *Observer* 24 December 2006 that some parents opposed the vaccination against cervical cancer as they felt it would promote unprotected sex and send confusing messages to young people about the right age for girls to lose their virginity. Since then a Catholic school in Greater Manchester has decided to withdraw from the government's vaccination programme against cervical cancer for girls. They object to the vaccination on the grounds that it will promote sexual promiscuity.

Question

1. What role should schools have in health protection and should faith-based school be able to exempt their pupils from such a programme?

The social and political context of faith schools

There are currently around seven thousand faith schools in England, six hundred secondary and six thousand four hundred primary institutions. Taylor (2005) estimated that the vast majority (6,955) are Christian, with 36 Jewish, 5 Muslim and 2 Sikh schools. However, due to the emphasis of current government policy these figures are probably an understatement. At the same time as the number of faith schools are increasing, the numbers of individuals who worship on a regular basis is in steady decline. The decline in churchgoing is a long-term problem that affects almost all faiths. For instance, only 6.3 per cent of the population attend church on a regular basis and of these 29 per cent are over the age of 65 (BBC, 2006).

The Times, for example, reports that:

> Estimates for worshipers in 2006, based on previous years' figures suggest 861,800 Catholics attend mass every Sunday, compared with 893,100 in 2005, while 852,500 Anglicans went to Sunday services last year, down 18, 100 on 2005. (*Times*, 2007)

Activity

1. Carry out a small-scale survey to find out why people do not attend church.
2. Make the group you survey as socially, ethnically as diverse as you can. You should also take gender and class into account when undertaking this task.
3. Present your findings in a poster.

Societal attitudes to faith schools

However, it should be noted though that some faith groups, such as Muslims, do not exhibit the same pattern of decline, these only represent a small percentage of the total population. Along with the decline in religious participation there also appears to be an opposition to state support for faith-based schools. In an opinion poll carried out for the *Guardian* (12 August–14 August 2005), it was found that two-thirds of the population opposed funding of faith-based schools. There was also an element of discrimination in the findings as 8 per cent of the population were quite happy for there to be funding for Christian and Jewish schools, but not the equivalent funding for Muslim schools.

Religious discrimination

The opposition to Muslim schools also highlights an important development within British society over the past 50 or more years. British society has changed with mass immigration from, initially, those parts of the world that were once part of the British Empire. This change to British society as a result of such population movements has produced increased difference and diversity in terms of culture, language, religious faith and ethnicity. It would seem almost ironic that the government has decided to pursue a policy of increasing schools of a religious nature against this background of growing secularism and the development of a multicultural society. It should also be noted that there is a growing inequality within the UK. The gap between the richest and the poorest has been growing, for the most part, over the past 30 years under both the previous Conservative administration and especially the New Labour government (Peston, 2008). Issues such as the decline of churchgoing, increased social diversity and the parallel increase in social inequalities all impact on education, producing winners and losers, out of which the privileged continue to achieve within the school system. One of the key responses by the government to this recurring problem has been to promote faith schools.

Government policy

Government policy in education can be explained in terms of the dominant economic, social and political policies of the philosophical doctrine of 'neo-liberalism'. In terms of public services such as education, this has resulted in the increasing prevalence of account-ability through the use of targets and the measurement of performance, both of individuals and institutions. Theoretically at least, the use of competition is promoted to reduce the cost of public services while, magically, increasing the quality of provision. In other words, such policy involves the education service replicating the practices of private industry and thus becoming a market (Ball, 2007; Cole, 2006). The market requires a diversity of suppliers and notion of choice for the consumer. The commitment to the market, with its stress on con-sumer choice as the mechanism for the distribution of resources, has recently led to some faith groups demanding the right to their own schools.

Thus, the current increase in faith schools has resulted from a number of diverse factors. Partly, it is to do with the impact of government neo-liberal policy and the restructuring of the education system, especially within the secondary phase of education. The other issue that is driving the demand for more faith-based schools is the failure of the education sys-tem to meet the needs of different minority ethnic groups.

New Labour's support for faith schools

The Labour Party's conversion to support faith schools is comparatively recent move. The Party's commitment in the early 1980s was to a school system that was by its nature inclu-sive based on the needs of the majority of ordinary children. This can be evidenced by their attitude to private education. In a Party pamphlet on Private Schools published in 1980 they state:

> . . . under a Labour Government. Policies for combating privilege in education are part of a demo-cratic socialist assault on privilege, wealth, power and influence in our society. We are confident that these policies, together with our determination to improve standards of opportunity and provision throughout the maintained sector, will have the effect of bringing major and irreversible change to the structure of our society and the continuing advancement of the interests of working people and their families. (Labour Party, 1980: 50)

However, since this declaration of commitment to equal opportunities and inclusion, New Labour has taken on the legacy of the neo-liberal marketization of education, extend-ing choice with a new ingredient: faith. The 2001 Education Act (DfES, 2001) signalled an enthusiastic commitment to non-Christian faith schools and was designed to increase their number. New Labour's commitment to faith schools of all types is not limited to choice mechanisms, but is rather linked to the idea that the social ethos of a faith school will provide an increase in social capital and hence improved level of educational attainment

(Gamarnikov and Green, 2005). In this climate, competition is now in itself, not enough. Faith is the so-called magic bullet that will see a 'world class' education system develop out of all-pervasive neo-liberal structures. The needs of pupils from working-class or minority ethnic backgrounds can thus be seen to evaporate in the heady air of targets, standards, markets and faith.

Stop, Read and Reflect

Pick an area known to you and identify the faith schools in the locality. Obtain as much information about these schools, for instance, admissions policies, number of children who have free school meals through using their websites and Ofsted school reports.

Compare the data you have collected with the census data freely available on the web, and answer the following questions.

Questions

1. Do the profiles of the schools you have identified match the socio-economic demographic profile of the locality it is situated in? Can you explain why the profile matches or does not match?
2. Go through the same process with a poor or affluent locality that is different from the one you have already studied: are the results the same or different? Can you explain why? What conclusions do you draw from your research?

Racism and educational failure

The response to mass immigration on the part of the education system has grown through a number of stages since the 1950s. The initial phase was one of assimilation, which was primarily aimed at the newly settled community for the Indian subcontinent. During this phase the Afro-Caribbean community was largely ignored and was deemed not to have any particular needs as the focus rested the purpose of speaking English (Mullard, 1982). The failure of assimilation resulted in, what has been termed, the integrationist model that came into being in the 1960s. In reality, this model of dealing with minority ethnic groups produced recognition of cultural difference, which was often tokenistic and frequently referred to as the three Ss: Saris, Samosas and Steel Bands. The events of the early and mid-1980s – (riots in Brixton, Liverpool and Bristol), put paid to this approach to education. Thereafter, a policy of cultural pluralism was adopted and there was some recognition of racism within the education system. However, since the late 1980s, and especially since the events of 11 September 2001 and 7 July 2005, the model that is being used again is one of assimilation. In the process there is yet again a failure to recognize the needs of minority ethnic pupils who are being continually failed by the system.

Ethnic minority educational attainment

There remains a persistent and general dissatisfaction among minority ethnic groups of the levels of achievement exhibited by their children. This is especially true in the Afro-Caribbean community (Richardson, 2005; Gillborn, 2008) who are reported as suffering disproportionately high levels of exclusion. The Afro-Caribbean community, similar to other groups who are being failed and suffer racism, is not demanding a right to faith schools, but rather cultural recognition. In his study on the future of multicultural Britain, Parekh (2000) identified education as one of the key issues facing Muslim communities. The system is not just failing children in terms of educational achievement but in relation to their general social needs. The issue of being recognized within the curriculum has been persistently argued for by parents since the Scarmen Report (1981) into the Brixton riots. While to some degree, faith schools provide for cultural recognition, the majority of Muslim parents, and indeed parents from other minority ethnic groups, do not in fact want faith-based schools, but a more effective education system that recognizes their needs (Madood et al., 1994). In many ways, the increased demand for Islamic schools can be viewed as a direct response to the increase in Islamophobia that is prevalent in society – (of which there are many examples, not least from middle-class writers such as Martin Amis and Rod Liddle). The retreat into culturally safe environs or enclaves such as faith schools is not so dissimilar to the movement in the 1970s by Afro-Caribbean youths to adopt Rastafarianism as a method of reclaiming dignity in the face of the unwarranted racism.

The beneficiaries of faith schools

Those who seek to defend faith schools frequently attack the idea that they have become the repositories of status and privilege for the middle classes (Odone, 2008). Yet this is despite the fact that evidence often supports just such a contention (Ball, 2008). West and Hind (2003) in a study on school admissions systems found that 10 per cent of voluntary aided schools reported interviewing parents and 16 per cent interviewing pupils, as part of their admissions procedures. Interviewing as part of the admission to a secondary school is against the government's code of practice. They also found that a significant minority of voluntary aided and foundation schools used a variety of criteria to select-in and select-out groups of pupils. The criteria used included

> children of employees; children of former pupils; partial selection by ability/aptitude in a subject area or by general ability; and children with a family connection to the school. (West and Hind, 2003: 3)

In a study on the achievement levels of pupils of faith schools (Gibbons and Silva, 2006), it was found that faith schools at the primary level offered only a tiny advantage of around one percentile point in achievement over non-faith schools, in the results produced for Key

Stage 2 SATs tests. Gibbons and Silva also found that:

> Any benefit of attending a Faith school is linked to the more autonomous admission and govern-ance arrangements that characterised 'Voluntary Aided' schools....Pupils in religiously affiliated schools where admissions were under the control of the Local Education Authority ('Voluntary Controlled' schools) do not progress faster than pupils in Secular primary schools. (2006: 2)

In another study of faith-based schools the admissions procedures included the require-ment of a reference from a priest/minister/religious leader to confirm that the information provided by the parents was indeed accurate. 'Eight out of ten...sought information on church attendance; half on involvement in the church and a third asked for proof that a child's reli-gious milestones, such as baptism or first Holy Communion had taken place' (Pennell et al., 2007). In a study on the best performing 200 state comprehensives by the Sutton Trust (2006), it was found that even those schools that were located in areas of low socio-economic status had far fewer students who were entitled to free school dinners – a key indicator of poverty. While not all the schools were faith-based schools, a significant number were.

Selection and achievement

From the evidence of these studies, it would seem that higher levels of achievement in faith schools is not always related to the idea of equality upon which their very concept and promo-tion is predicated. Rather, it could be argued that the levels of attainment exhibited by their pupils are in fact a function of the selective process of admissions procedures, rather than anything the schools actually do. It might be suggested that social segregation is the real func-tion of faith schools. For example, in a further study on school admissions (Tough and Brooks, 2007), it was concluded that schools should not be allowed to be their own admission author-ities as it leads insidiously to practices that negatively impact on certain groups of pupils iden-tified by the school as not being worthy or of the sort they want. In the context of a system that is competitively driven, it would make perfect sense for schools to discriminate against pupils with special needs, language issues or any other educational need that would seem to impact on their ability to achieve government-inspired targets. Provision for such children would incur extra cost in terms of the need for supporting resources, and their levels of attainment would obviously impact on the schools' position in national league tables, which would, in turn, affect the popularity of the school. Thus, rather than faith schools contributing to social cohesion it would, in fact, seem they are more likely to contribute to social segregation.

The child

While this is not the place to embark on a lengthy discussion of the rights of the child it is an issue that should be discussed in the context of faith education. Pring (2005) argues that the very basis of faith schools is contrary to the aims of education and the development of autonomous individuals, for their principal aim is to indoctrinate the child into the faith. Defenders of the faith school will typically justify this emphasis in terms of parental rights, closely followed by ethos and academic achievement (see discussion above). However, the rights of the child in this context become secondary to the rights and interests of parents. This implies that the child is little more than the property of the parent. As Marples (2005) points out, it is one thing to recognize that parenthood can bring profound satisfaction and fulfilment, but quite another to conclude that the interests of parents and children are coincidental, for this is wrong! The interests of the child lie in being able to develop her/his own understanding of the world, ultimately in ways that allow the development of their own moral code. Thus, the very notion of parental rights needs to be challenged, since children are not objects. As Archard (2003: 65) points out, parents have duties:

> although it may be in a child's interest to be brought up within a family by parents, it is not clear that adults have rights over their own children....an influential, but mistaken, view of natural parents as somehow owners of those children they produce....parents have, rather than parental rights, duties to care for their children and discretion in their discharge.

Stop, Read and Reflect

Charles Fried argues that:

- The right to form one's child's values [is an extension of] the basic right not to be interfered with in doing these things for oneself
- The child is regarded as an extension of the self. (MacMullen, 2007)

Questions

1. How does this view of the child conflict with the notion of children's rights?
2. Do these views support the right of parents to send their children to faith schools more than any idea of children's rights?

It might be expected that in the normal course of family interaction a child would usually share the interests and rituals of parents and the family. However, this does not mean that a parent has the automatic right to mould their child (Marples, 2005). In sharing all manner of things with the child, parents should not seek to determine or close down the prospects for their offspring, but rather allow for a more open future that naturally unfolds (Feinberg, 1980). The very notion of the faith school, to ensure subsequent generations continue the faith, would seem to stand in direct opposition to the aim of promoting an open future. The rights of the individual to refuse to be inducted into a faith, with due consideration and mature reflection, are unduly ignored as they are seen to extend beyond the ability of the child.

Conclusion

In a society that is increasingly secular, the growth of faith schools can be regarded as a largely cynical attempt by government to shore up a market-based approach to education. This is achieved by appealing to the religious beliefs of some parents and by co-opting others into accepting the rhetoric of neo-liberal policy, via the myth that faith schools are adept to promote achievement. At the same time, such policy and practice is systematically failing to meet the needs of children that are continually disadvantaged by the education system. One only has to read studies such as Evans (2006) or the chapters by Mufti and Wrigley in this volume to see that current government policy is failing the very children it claims to be helping. In terms of ethnic minority pupils, the chapter by Garratt and Piper in this volume also provides a vivid example of similar benign neglect. However, those faith organizations that are already established in the educational market place are taking control of increasing numbers of schools in a bid to influence the education of our children. The clearest example of this is the expansion of the number of Academies run by the Vardy foundation, a Christian fundamentalist educational charity, which proposes to set up even more of the same institutions in the very near future.

Contemporary issues and faith schools

The major issues that face contemporary education, such as racism and the benign neglect of working-class children, are frequently glossed over by forms of policy rhetoric that clearly favour the interests of the middle class. In this respect, the education system is effectively being modernized back into a Victorian future (Ball, 2008). However, it is unlikely that the currently fragmented school system, in part defined by the business interests of multiple faith groups, will ever be capable of providing the sort of education that ordinary children need. On the contrary, the policy of faith schools is in fact creating a segregated system that does little to address the agenda towards social inclusion, but instead opens a gaping chasm of social and economic division based on social class. In fact, one has only to examine the admissions policies on faith schools to observe the compelling raft of evidence. Nevertheless, the myth of the superiority of faith schools over their secular cousins is continued through the relentless pursuit of iniquitous and socially divisive policies.

While many raise concerns about the influence that faith groups have over education and the fragmentation and segregation they bring to the system, under the constraints of current social and educational policy, a truly secular school remains a political impossibility. To conclude, perhaps the most disturbing factor about the continuous growth of faith school policy is the neglect of the child in terms of her/his rights to freedom of expression; that is, the freedom to be allowed to grow and develop as an independent and autonomous individual free of the shackles of indoctrination. Like many of this government's policies in education, the (every) child (that matters) appears to have gone missing (Murphy et al., 2006).

Key Points

- Current education policy is committed to the expansion of the number of faith schools
- Faith-based institutions operate at all levels of the education system
- All schools are required by law to engage in a broadly Christian act of worship whether they are faith based or not. There are no completely secular schools in the state sector
- As the number of faith schools are increasing, the number of individuals attending church or other religious service is decreasing – except within the Muslim community
- The UK is becoming an increasingly diverse society: ethnically, culturally, socially and linguistically
- Faith-based schools are increasingly able to control their own admissions system
- Research evidence suggests that those schools that control their own admissions systems discriminate against those defined as outsiders. The outsiders are often the most disadvantaged in society
- Schools that control their admissions perform better academically than those that do not
- The expansion of the faith sector is part of the Academies initiative, which is in effect the privatization of schools
- Large sections of society are opposed to faith schools – this opposition increases if the faith of the school in question is Muslim
- Faith-based education ignores the right of the child not to be indoctrinated.

Further Reading

David Archard (2004) *Children, Family and the State*, Aldershot: Ashgate.

Roy Gardner, Jo Cairns and Denis Lawton (2005) *Faith Schools Consensus or Conflict?*, London: Routledge.

Tariq Modood (2005) *Multicultural Politics Racism, Ethnicity and Muslims in Britain*, Edinburgh: University of Edinburgh Press.

Marie Parker-Jenkins, Dimitra Hartas and Barrie Irving (2005) *In Good Faith Schools, Religion and Public Funding*, Aldershot: Ashgate.

References

Archard, D. (2003) *Children, Family and Naïve State*, Aldershot: Ashgate.

Asthana (2007) *Crisis of Faith in First Secular School*, Observer 23 September 2007 www.guardian.co.uk/uk/2007/sep/23/schools.faithschools [accessed 4 July 2008].

Ball, S. (2007) *Education PLC: Understanding Private Sector Participation in Public Sector Education*, London: Routledge.

Ball, S. (2008) *The Education Debate*, London: Polity Press.

BBC (2006) *Minorities Prop Up Church-Going*, BBC, 18 September, http://news.bbc.co.uk/1/hi/uk/5349132.stm [accessed 4 July 2008].

Brighouse, H. (2005) 'Faith-based schools in the United Kingdom: an unenthusiastic defence of a slightly reformed status quo', in R. Gardner, J Cairns and D. Lawton (eds), *Faith Schools: Consensus or Conflict*, London: RoutledgeFalmer.

Cole, M. (2006) 'New Labour, globalisation and social justice: the role of teacher education', in D. Kassem, E. Mufti and J. Robinson (eds), *Education Studies: Issues and Critical Perspectives*, Maidenhead: Open University Press.

Cush, D. (2003) 'Should the state fund schools with a religious character?' *Professional Council for Religious Education (PCfRE)*, 25 (2): 10–15.

Cush, D. (2005) 'The faith schools debate', *British Journal of Sociology of Education*, 26 (3): 435–42.

Department for Children, Schools and Families (DCSF) (2007) *Faith in the System*, London: DCSF.

Department for Education and Skills (DfES) (2001) *Schools: Building on success*, London: The Stationery Office.

Evans, G. (2006) *Educational Failure and Working Class White Children*, London: Palgrave Macmillan.

Feinberg, J. (1980) 'The child's right to open future', in W. Aiken and H. LaFollette (eds), *Whose Child? Children's Rights, Parental Authority, and State Power*, Totowa: Littlefield, Adams & Co.

Gamarnikov, E. and Green, A. (2005) 'Keeping faith with school capital: from Coleman to New Labour on social justice, religion and education', in R. Gardner, J Cairns and D. Lawton (eds), *Faith Schools: Consensus or Conflict*, London: RoutledgeFalmer.

Gibbons, S. and Silva, O. (2006) 'Faith primary schools: better schools or better pupils?' London: Centre for the Economics of Education/London School of Economics.

Gillborn, D. (2008) *Racism and Education: Coincidence or Conspiracy?* London: Routledge.

Harris, J. (2005) 'What a creation…', *Guardian*, 15 January, www.guardian.co.uk/books/2005/jan/15/features.politics [accessed 4 July 2008].

Jackson, R. (2003) 'Should the state fund faith-based schools? A review of the arguments', *British Journal of Religious Education*, 25 (2): 89–102.

Labour Party (1980) *Private Schools: A Labour Party Discussion Document*, London: Labour Party.

Madood, T., Beishon, S. and Virdec, S. (1994) *Changing Ethnic Identities*, London: Policy Studies Institute.

Marples, R. (2005) 'Against faith schools: a philosophical argument for children's rights', *International Journal of Children's Spirituality*, 10 (2): 133–47.

McGettrick, B. (2005) 'Perceptions and practices of Christian schools', in R. Gardner, J Cairns and D. Lawton (eds), *Faith Schools: Consensus or Conflict*, London: RoutledgeFalmer.

MacMullen, I. (2007) *Faith in Schools*, Princeton: University of Princeton Press.

Mullard, C. (1982) 'Multiracial education in Britain: from assimilation to cultural pluralism', in J. Tierney (ed.), *Race, Migration and Schooling*, London: Holt Education.

Murphy, L., Kassem, D. and Fenwick, G. (2006) 'The politics of the National Literacy and Numeracy Strategies', in D. Kassem, E. Mufti and J. Robinson (eds), *Education Studies Issues and Critical Perspectives*, Maidenhead: Open University Press.

Odone, C. (2008) *In Bad Faith: The New Betrayal of Faith School*, London: Centre for Policy Studies.

Parekh, B. (2000) *The Future of Multi-Ethnic Britain*, London: Profile Books.

Parker-Jenkins, M., Hartas, D. and Irving, B. (2005) *In Good Faith: Schools, Religion and Public Funding*, Aldershot: Ashgate.

Pennell, H., West, A. and Hind, A.(2007) *Religious Composition and Admission Processes of Faith Secondary Schools in London*, London: Education Research Group/London School of Economics and Political Science.

Peston, R. (2008) *Who Runs Britain? How the Super-Rich are Changing Our Lives*, London: Hodder & Stoughton.

Pring, R. (2005) 'Are faith schools justified?' in R. Gardner, J. Cairns and D. Lawton (eds), *Faith Schools: Consensus or Conflict*, London: RoutledgeFalmer.

Richardson, B. (2005) *Tell It Like It is: How Our Schools Fail Black Children*, London: Bookmarks Publications.

Sutton Trust (2006) *The Social Composition of Top Comprehensive Schools: Rates of Eligibility for Free School Diners at 200 Highest Performing Comprehensive Schools*, London: Sutton Trust.

Taylor, M. (2005) 'Two thirds oppose state aided faith schools', *Guardian*, 23 August, www.guardian.co.uk/uk/2005/aug/23/schools.faithschools [accessed 4 July 2008].

Times (2007) 'Anglican Church attendance has stabilised', *Times Online*, 23 December 2007 www.timesonline.co.uk/tol/comment/faith/article3089229.ece [accessed 4 July 2008].

Tough, S. and Brooks, R. (2007) *School Admissions: Fair Choice for Parents and Pupils*, London: IPPR.

West, A. and Hind, A. (2003) *Secondary School Admissions in England: Exploring the Extent of Overt and Covert Selection*, London: Research and Information on State Education/London School of Economics.

White working-class kids: Why are they failing?

Emmanuel Mufti

6

Introduction

Education is not an uncontested enterprise, for every success within the system there are corresponding numbers that fail to succeed at recommended levels. In fact, there is a well-known correlation between social factors and levels of educational success (Murphy et al., 2008) at all levels of the UK system. While gender and ethnicity can, and do, play a part in determining levels of educational success, the overwhelming challenge facing today's education system is associated with widening differentials in relation to the social class system. Although the mainstream media ensures that the issue of gender specific achievement remains firmly within the public consciousness, it is worth noting that achievement differentials based upon social class are three times greater than those relating to gender. In terms of white British Children, there is a 9 per cent achievement gap at General Certificate of Secondary Education (GCSE) in relation to gender but a 33 per cent achievement gap in terms of those who receive free school meals and those who do not (DfES, 2007). The latter is important in so far as free school meals are often used as an indicator of social class when discussing educational issues. Thus, it is significant to note that in 2006, while 61 per cent of children not receiving free school meals were able to achieve 5 A–C grades at GCSE, only 33 per cent of those actually receiving free school meals achieved at the same level (DfES, 2007). In further examining the issue, we discover that only 15 per cent of white working-class boys achieved the above noted level of success, compared with a healthier 45 per cent of boys from higher socio-economic groupings. These differentials are not merely limited to achievement at GCSE level, for similar examples can be found at all levels of formal education from the foundation stage to university entry. Indeed, it is evidence such as this that led Trevor Phillips to suggest that white working-class British boys, in particular, are often the victims of an unfair and unjust system (2008).

However, this issue is certainly not new. For example, Halsey et al. (1980) comprehensively outline the impact of social class and parental status upon corresponding levels of educational achievement. Furthermore, as Steedman (1985) pointed out, the disjuncture between how children 'ought to be' and how working-class children actually 'are' has been noted since the 1880s. This latter point leads us to the main issue relating to the achievement of white working-class children: namely, who determines what children 'ought to be' and what is this concept based upon?

Defining the class system

Within the UK, definitions of class are primarily based on the analytic category of occupation, along with academic qualifications, rather than any actual measure of income. Typically, the social class of a child will largely depend on the occupation and qualification levels of primarily the father. Children are placed into categories according to the occupation, where applicable, of their fathers. The classifications are as follows:

The National Statistics Socio-economic Classification Analytic Classes

1. Higher managerial and professional occupations
   a. Large employers and higher managerial occupations
   b. Higher professional occupations
2. Lower managerial and professional occupations
3. Intermediate occupations
4. Small employers and own account workers
5. Lower supervisory and technical occupations
6. Semi-routine occupations
7. Routine occupations
8. Never worked and long-term unemployed.

Class and educational attainment

However, while the above categories provide a definition of the class system they do little to explore the reasons why such differentials exist between the classes when it comes to educational achievement. Furthermore, they tend to mask the relationships that exist between various divisions of social classification. In this way, each of the above listed groups does not live in social isolation but is rather connected through a series of social relationships; that is, relationships that Marxist theory would determine as working primarily in favour of those situated in so-called higher categories of social classification, as depicted in the table. In addition, criticism has been levelled at them for being too crude and simplistic, for example, in grouping large-scale employers with, say, those owning small businesses and employing a small number of workers. Further issues around the way they increase the range of social classifications, and separate what Marx would have recognized as the working class into a number of different sub categories, has produced sharp criticism. Some have argued that it provides the opportunity to suggest that forms of discrimination faced by the working class will be different at different putative levels. Yet this separation can only ultimately lead to less strength when it comes to fighting for equality (Hill and Cole, 2001). Theses issues will be picked up again and discussed in more detail throughout the chapter.

Free School Meal Pupils Underachieve

Only 176, or just over half a per cent, of nearly 30,000 pupils who got three good A levels were eligible for free school meals…household income is the single biggest predictor of a child's academic success.

Just over thirteen per cent of children qualify for free school meals up to the age of sixteen…. figures reveal the high drop-out rates: nearly 80,000 of 16-year-olds received free school meals two years ago but only 5,096 went on to do A levels, though more went into vocational training. (*Guardian*, 23 February 2008)

In a report in the *Guardian* it was claimed that only 3 per cent of children who have had free school meals go on to obtain three good A levels.

Schools and social class

It is interesting to note that at the level of the school within the education system the above classifications are rarely used as markers of social class. Instead, the most common criterion used as an indication of class in terms of schooling is eligibility for free school meals.

It is in this respect that we tend to hear the terms socio-economic status rather than class utilized. Thus, while it may seem a mere matter of semantics to refer to the concept of socio-economic status rather than class itself, the shift in meaning does have the effect of moving the emphasis towards the individual and diverting the focus away from the notion of 'group'. At times this can be problematic to a more detailed discussion, since individual success or failure is much easier to explain (while maintaining the illusion of meritocracy), than any large-scale failure of any particular section of society. Ultimately, then, if status is determined by one's socio-economic standing then theoretically, with the right education, opportunities and advancement, it must be possible to improve one's position in society. However, as will be argued throughout this chapter, and indeed as the statistics in the introduction suggest, this is not as simple or straightforward as it first appears. As Willis (1977: 128) stated:

> Insofar as knowledge is always biased and shot through with class, meaning the working class student must overcome his inbuilt disadvantage of possessing the wrong class culture and the wrong educational decoders to start with, a few can make it. The class can never follow. It is through a good number trying, however, that the class structure is legitimated.

What Willis is arguing is that to maintain the illusion of equality of opportunity and meritocracy, as suggested by consensus theorists, some children from working-class backgrounds will inevitably have to achieve and be successful. However, the system will usually ensure that the numbers succeeding will be heavily restricted, thus serving to perpetuate and maintain society's structural inequalities.

Culture

The UK media is quick to comment on the shape and form of culture within and among the working class, albeit usually in a somewhat negative fashion. Consider headlines, for example, around the rise of gang culture, street culture, gun and knife culture and the pervasive influence of the benefit culture. We can further extend the term to include issues of class culture and how that manifests itself across certain sectors of society. The issue of culture is thus one that can be seen to permeate modern life and pervade the discourse around social groupings, filtering into mainstream political debate. As Kuper (1999: 1) states:

> Politicians urge cultural revolution. Apparently a seismic cultural change is needed to resolve the problems of poverty, drug abuse, crime, illegitimacy, and industrial competitiveness. There is talk about cultural difference between the sexes and the generations, between football teams, or between advertising agencies.

Such rhetoric suggests there are a number of different cultures currently operating simultaneously in England. Of course, not all have equal status and it would be naïve to suggest they do. This is especially true in relation to Phillips' (2008) point that white working-class children can be regarded as a disadvantaged group. Indeed, it is the issue of how particular diverse cultures interact with one another, and the extent to which they enjoy equal access to opportunities and notions of success, that is of key importance to this chapter.

Cultural conflict

Somewhat ironically, Evans (2006) suggests that cultures that should actually work together have in fact been pitched against each other. So rather than examining their similarities as oppressed groups, the white working-class and Pakistani community, for example, will often focus upon their differences and grievances towards one another, and thus overlook the inequalities of an unjust system that disadvantages both groups/communities. This can lead to more general critical discussion around the theme of inequality being sidetracked and distorted by issues of immigration and cultural conflict among disadvantaged groups. It is when Evans (ibid.) discusses the issue of the white working class that we are able to see how culture and difference negatively merge to impact upon the expectations that different cultural groups possess towards the 'Other'.

Socialization

Evans states that there is a fundamental difference between the actions and attitudes of white working-class boys in particular, both in and away from the home environment. The flipside of culture is that when we accept the basic premise of socialization/enculturation, we can see how individuals would feel pressured to adopt the cultural characteristics of the group to which they are designated and ostensibly belong. However, the development and expectations of cultural groups, and their explicit patterns of behaviour, are not always part of a natural process. Nor, for that matter, are they fully determined or constructed by the individuals that constitute those groups. Significantly, the influence and role of the media can impact upon how cultural groups tend to be perceived, where, in turn, such perceptions can alter the behavioural expectations of those both within and outside a particular group. Popular television shows and their characters, such as Vicky Pollard in *Little Britain*, show a stereotypical view of young white working-class culture, which is further reinforced by more traditional commentary around anti-social behaviour within working-class communities and schools. Evans (2006) suggests that these elements can, in some cases, lead white working-class children to fulfil the behaviour that is expected of them in places outside the home environment, such as the school. The nature of such self-fulfilling prophesies can mean that some individuals and groups are influenced to adopt practices that inevitably clash with the dominant cultural regime within schools, producing marked cultural dissonance and acute disengagement.

Activity

1. Consider how you would expect the following groups to act within an educational setting such as a school:
   - White working-class boys
   - White middle-class girls
   - Middle-class boys
   - Middle-class girls
   - Afro-Caribbean children.
2. Can you explain your expectations? If you are thinking of becoming a teacher how do you think this might impact on your teaching?

Theoretical perspectives

The issue of social class manifests itself within the education system in a variety of complex ways. One useful tool to examine this complexity can be found in Bourdieu's (1977) theory of cultural capital, linked to the concept of habitus. For Bourdieu (ibid.) these concepts can be employed to explain why and how certain students are more comfortable with, and, therefore, more likely to succeed in the education system. According to his theory, schools are a more natural environment for certain children, whose parents and families, with privileged insight, are more able to promote the value of education, passing on their wisdom and experience and appropriate forms of 'capital'. Children from more privileged families are thus more likely to gain a head start on those less fortunate, since their 'habitus' (i.e. their core values, dispositions and interests) and cultural capital can be seen to align more closely with the dominant traditions, rituals and routines that govern practice within schools. Schools are places that naturally value a willingness to learn and readily reward appropriate forms of behaviour from children in their care. Those who are more willing or, indeed able (in terms of cultural capital) to comply with the practices that characterize formal schooling will quite obviously be more disposed to integrating smoothly and successfully into schools. It is for these reasons, that not all groups in society perform equally well within the education system. Some children are far less likely to succeed if, for example, their parents' academic qualifications are low, or if they lack the requisite experience or 'know-how', and it is this type of inequality within the system that Bourdieu (ibid.) seeks to explain.

Cultural capital

For Bourdieu, (1977) there are three main types of cultural capital that an individual may bring to an educational environment: *embodied*, *institutionalized* and *objective*. The *embodied* state includes the investment of time and takes account of the influence of primary carers, typically parents. The *institutionalized* form recognizes the value of educational qualifications and achievements and, finally, the *objective* form notes the significance of cultural goods such as books, resources and places to study, 'similar to concepts of material deprivation or affluence' (Reay et al., 2005: 20). The theory suggests that those who are most likely to succeed tend to come to education from families which have previously succeeded within the education system, and that furthermore the education system is primarily created, maintained and staffed by those who have done the same.

Due to the influences identified above, the cultural capital that children from more privileged groups bring to education can result in them gaining a distinct advantage. As noted above, this is because the value systems, behavioural expectations and types of knowledge that are deemed to be important within schools are also similar to those they will encounter at home. Of course this also results in the opposite being true for children from groups which have not succeeded as well within education and who, therefore, do not necessarily view (academic) success with quite the same pride and enthusiasm. In essence, the illusion of meritocracy is maintained as each individual receives a similar education and similar opportunities to succeed through exams but there is a fundamental advantage for those children whose cultural capital is more in tune with the ethos and culture of the school. As Bourdieu (1977) suggested, when the capital of a student links well with the field of an educational environment then this person can feel like 'a fish in water'. However, when there is dissonance or disjuncture between them it can lead to feelings of isolation, discomfort and insecurity.

The hidden curriculum and conflict theorists

Earlier in the chapter we examined how issues of culture and difference can potentially lead to conflict. This is not always, and in reality is rarely, a form of conflict between groups with similar status. When considering whose culture is most prominent in the school system, it is easy to discern it is not that which white working-class children would willingly take to be their own. Instead, the dominant culture is developed and imposed by those in positions of power, many of whom have previously succeeded in the education system. Through a series of barriers, such as the ones discussed here and above, this culture works to deliberately exclude certain sections of society from achieving success, and in the process serves to maintain and perpetuate marked social divisions. From a conflict perspective (see Marx, for example), many of the ways in which schools fail certain children is through the *institutionalization* of official knowledge (Apple, 2004), mediated through the curriculum, its content and teaching methods employed. Not to be lightly dismissed, this usefully illustrates the authority and pervasive influence of the dominant values embedded within, and employed through, education, and which effectively informs the intellectual basis of arguments developed by the conflict theorists.

Acceptable behaviour

However, while the official curriculum is of particular importance to the ways in which children are socialized and learn, the types of behaviour that are commonly expected and rewarded (and which are often class and gender related), are often more effectively mediated through the 'hidden curriculum' (Jackson, 1968). The hidden curriculum can be regarded as the sum total of messages gained from an educational experience, which do not, at least implicitly, form part of the official curriculum. Therefore, while there are no actual lessons in appropriate forms of gendered behaviour, understanding and respecting forms of hierarchy and authority within schools, and/or that academic knowledge is something to learn rather than create, we nevertheless take these and many more messages away from our educational experiences. Meighan and Siraj-Blatchford (2007) provide a more detailed list of messages students gain through the hidden curriculum. These include issues such as adults being more important than children, the Western world being more advanced and superior to the rest of the world and that the passive acceptance of ideas is more desirable than any form of intellectual criticism. The hidden curriculum therefore is not necessarily a simple and unintended by-product of the process of formal schooling. It can be viewed as a deliberate attempt to maintain social order through a series of covert and overt messages. That is, messages that can manifest themselves in numerous, myriad ways through: teachers' attitudes; admonishment and praise; classroom organization, layout and display; uniform requirements; prizes and punishments; and the elements and contents of school reports. In short, the ethos and direction of a school will be clearly defined through a series of messages constantly reinforced in actions, words and institutional arrangements.

The correspondence principle

The much admired and equally criticized work of Bowles and Gintis (1976) further developed the concept of the hidden curriculum, linking it to what they termed the 'correspondence principle'. Bowles and Gintis stated that the messages received by pupils via the hidden curriculum in schools correspond closely with the culture they will later encounter in the world of work. This is what Hatcher (2001) has referred to as the 'capitalist agenda for schools', in so far as part of the purpose of education is to create subservient workers within a capitalist economy. Such workers will have the necessary knowledge to be productive, but far more importantly the capacity to consider the working milieu as a natural and unchangeable environment, which they should work within rather than seek to alter.

For Bowles and Gintis, education corresponded with the world of work in a number of significant ways. First, their study revealed that grades related more to subservient personality traits than any actual level of ability, where compliance assured success. Secondly, like the world of work, schools were seen to operate hierarchically with a clearly defined chain of command and authority: teachers being in charge of pupils, deputies and heads in charge of teachers. Bowles and Gintis claim that an uncritical acceptance of these power relations will smooth the educational progress of compliant pupils much as it would within a work environment with compliant employees. The idea of external rewards through the exam system and their role in assisting the procurement of higher status employment also links the world of work to school. In the same way that much employment is unsatisfying and unrewarding, with only the prospect of a wage making it seem worthwhile, the learning process is seen as equally unrewarding with many children failing to enjoy school. However, in terms of external rewards, the carrot remains in both contexts: in one case wages, the other exam results.

While the importance of the work of Bowles and Gintis should not be underestimated there are a number of criticisms pertaining to their work. Some of these focus upon their reasoning and research methodologies but perhaps a more telling criticism is levelled at the way in which they present children as uncritical and unquestioning, the docile bodies (Foucault, 1977) and passive adopters of the hidden curriculum. Moreover, bearing in mind that scholars like Bowles and Gintis have been framed as part of a tradition of conflict theorists within education, many have argued there is actually little evidence of any conflict within their work. This has led, for example, to Apple (1999) and Giroux (2001) criticizing their work as being somewhat misleading, although Bowles and Gintis (2001) have since rejected such claims.

Context and culture

In contrast, similar criticism could not be levelled at Paul Willis who, in his seminal text *Learning to Labour – How Working Class Kids Get Working Class Jobs* (1977), discovered strong evidence of a rejection of school and the formulation of a counter culture among working-class pupils. Willis followed a group of 12 boys for their last 18 months of school and into their first jobs. The 'lads', as Willis coined them, had clearly rejected the messages sent to them via the hidden and official curriculum. They had little respect for teachers and more subservient pupils ('earoles') and instinctively realized that the 'rewards' of good performance in school were simply not applicable to them, as they had no prospect of ever succeeding within the system. This was not as Willis states a politically aware decision, the racism and sexism of the 'lads' was, in fact, contrary to such an awareness, but instead the awareness was developed from observing those around them from similar backgrounds within their homes and wider community. In this case, their peers obtained jobs primarily in semi-skilled and unskilled labour, for which schools were regarded as having little or nothing to contribute towards. However, once Willis followed the 'lads' into their first jobs he discovered that what was classed as a 'counter culture' within schools actually reflected the dominant culture within those very workplaces. Therefore, the rejection of the school culture was borne out of it having little relevance to their own way of life (or what

Bourdieu (1977) recognized as 'habitus'). Quite perceptively, the 'lads' also realized that academic qualifications were unlikely to be achieved within such a divisive system, which Willis (1977) argued was developed to exclude and marginalize many of their 'class' from achieving and succeeding.

Moving forward

Throughout this volume, a range of new school systems such as Academies have been critiqued together with an examination of the testing régime and concept of school choice. A reading of these chapters will demonstrate that they have achieved little in narrowing the gap between various social groups, and in particular, those groupings defined in terms of class. This is not to suggest that politicians and policy developers are not aware of the issue but rather it questions whether their current strategies are sufficient to make a long and lasting difference?

Deficit model of education

In short, the rhetoric suggests not. For in response to the specific issue of white working-class boys' underachievement, politicians tend to focus upon a deficit model of education. That is, one that tends to pathologize children, suggesting they are falling behind due to their innate lack of ability as opposed to any notion that the system may have failed them. As one Liberal Democrat, David Laws, argues that:

> We need a massive targeted increase in funding for deprived young people, to allow more catch-up classes and additional support to give every child a chance. (Laws, 2008)

Or as the Conservative, Michael Goves (2008) contends:

> We need a school system that allows bright children to succeed regardless of their economic background. We can only achieve this by focusing on the basics like getting all children reading after two years of primary school. Instead we still have a system where the achievement gap between rich and poor pupils grows as they progress through their school careers.

What the above quotes demonstrate is that policy makers tend to see improvement in terms of minor tweaking, rather than as part of any radical and wide-scale systematic change. In contrast, Hill and Cole (2001) argue for the adoption and development of critical pedagogy within the school curriculum. This approach, as outlined by Giroux (1988), would move the curriculum away from the passively functional and more towards the actively critical. For example, it would provide an insight into many of the theoretical concepts contained within this chapter. Furthermore, it would provide a critique of the system allowing individuals to see how they are influenced (and oppressed) by dominant cultures and practices, and to explore ways in which to address aspects of difference and diversity. It would seek to debate the class system and lay it open to rigorous critique.

Stop, Read and Reflect

Parents protested today about the curriculum content within their local primary school. They were unhappy that the teacher had claimed there was a global conspiracy to ensure that their children would be very likely, within the current system of education, to underachieve. The parents, mainly from lower socio-economic groups stated that they felt it was 'setting up their children to fail' and 'giving them an excuse not to listen'. They further stated that the teacher had, through his lessons, suggested that they were 'not the same' as other groups in society and the only way to overcome this was to fully understand it.

Questions

1. Which of the perspectives would you most agree with that of the teachers or parents and why?
2. Do you think the parents are right to complain?
3. What would be included in a curriculum such as that outlined above?
4. Would it improve the chances of success for disadvantaged groups in society?

To adopt a critical pedagogy in schools would require a range of modifications and changes to be made to all current systems and practices. Currently, according to Giroux (1988) and others such as Apple (2004), schools and society impute more value and convey higher status to certain types of knowledge and behaviour. For example, the promotion of forms of high culture over low culture, in particular in relation to the languages (Bernstein, 1971) used within schools and how these collectively fail to reflect the diversity of linguistic conventions used within UK homes, can be seen to disadvantage certain minority groups. However, critical pedagogy should go further than simply raising awareness of these issues. It should actively seek to overcome them. Schools should respond more appropriately to local needs as opposed to addressing the whims and vagaries of a nationally set and standardized curriculum. Teachers too, should improve their awareness of the culture of the community in which they practice and serve, and attempt to link educational practice to local needs. In this respect, the nature of education and lifelong learning should become a consultative process involving members of the community and drawing inspiration from local issues and themes. Finally, teachers should work to encourage and instil a sense of optimism and hope, through a language of possibility which extends well beyond the narrow, performative metric of an exam-based system. This is meant neither to apportion, nor place, any blame at the feet of individual teachers, but rather suggest that within the current system practitioners have little flexibility to achieve radical change within the confines of the official curriculum.

Conclusion

We may not think of white British people, regardless of socio-economic status, as belonging to a minority group and in terms of sheer numbers alone, it is clear that they do not. However, in terms of their standing and status within society, and the likelihood of success within the education system, there is no doubt that the problems faced by white working-class people remain as one of the largest and most stubborn challenges facing contemporary society. Thus, in order to begin to narrow the gap between the classes, we need to move away from the rhetoric of piecemeal solutions, to consider more radically why the issue of inequality, rooted in class, continues to persist as a problem within the education system; that is, an historically recursive one that has existed from the moment of its very inception. At the beginning of the twenty-first century, we are currently no closer to an equal playing field than at any point in the recent past or, indeed, over the last sixty years. Therefore, it is now time that we begin to consider more radical alternatives to curriculum knowledge and pedagogy, in order to make a real impact and difference to the embattled lives of young white working-class children.

Elements of this chapter are adapted from Murphy et al. (2008).

Key Points

- Education is a contested enterprise
- Though gender and ethnicity play a role in educational success the key issue is social class
- Children who receive free school meals (a standard indicator of poverty) are more likely to fail educationally
- White working-class boys demonstrate greater levels of underachievement than any other group of children
- Definitions of social class are contested – some sociologists take the occupation and income of the head of household as an indicator of social class position in society
- Marxism takes a different view of social class – defining class in terms of an individual's relationship to the means of production
- A number of theorists argue that due to the class nature of society equal opportunity and meritocracy are illusory
- Culture is identified as a key issue and often used to explain differences in educational attainment
- Key theoretical concepts: cultural capital and habitus. These concepts are used to explain differences in attainment
- It is argued that children from privileged backgrounds have greater cultural capital – knowledge and experience due to their habitus – environment, that is, core values, dispositions and interests
- The ideas above are framed by notions of conflict which is rooted in a Marxist analysis
- A further extension of these ideas is the correspondence principle – which links the hidden curriculum directly to the world of work and the needs of industry – that children are schooled to accept their role in work through socialization that takes place in school

- A number of writers argue that working-class students reject this process through a strong identification with their own class culture
- An alternative approach to education is critical pedagogy which is rooted in the idea of empowering the individual and challenging power structures in society

Further Reading

Cassen, R. and Kingdon, G. (2007) *Tackling Low Educational Achievement*, York: Joseph Rowntree Foundation.

Evans, G. (2006) *Educational Failure and White Working Class Children in Britain*, Hampshire: Palgrave Macmillan.

Gillian Plummer (2000) *Failing Working Class Girls*, London: Trentham Books.

Willis, P. (1977) *Learning to Labour*, Hants: Saxon House.

References

Apple, M. (1999) *Power, Meaning, and Identity*, New York: Peter Lang.

Apple, M. (2004) *Ideology and Curriculum*, 3rd edition, London: RoutledgeFalmer.

Bernstein, B. (1971) *Class, Codes and Control*, London: Paladin.

Bourdieu, P. (1977) *Outline of a Theory of Practice*, Cambridge: Cambridge University Press.

Bowles, S. and Gintis, H. (2001) *Schooling in Capitalist America Revisited* e\Papers\JEP-paper\Sociology of Education.tex. www.umass.edu/preferen/gintis/soced.pdf [accessed 8 July 2008].

Department for Education and Skills (DfES) (2007) *Gender and Education: The Evidence on Pupils in England*, Nottingham: DfES.

Evans, G. (2006) *Educational Failure and White Working Class Children in Britain*, Hampshire: Palgrave Macmillan.

Foucault, M. (1977) *Discipline and Punish – the Birth of the Prison*, London: Penguin.

Giroux, H. (1988) *Schooling and Struggle: Critical Pedagogy in the Modern Age*, Minnesota: University of Minnesota Press.

Giroux, H. (2001) *Theory and Resistance in Education: Towards a Pedagogy for the Opposition*, Westport: Greenwood Press.

Goves, M. (2008) in BBC News (2008) 'White working class boys failing', http://news.bbc.co.uk/1/hi/education/7220683.stm [accessed 12 June 2008].

Halsey, A. H., Heath, A. F. and Ridge, J. M. (1980) *Origins and Destinations: Family, Class and Education in Modern Britain*, Oxford: Clarendon Press.

Hatcher, R. (2001) 'Getting down to business: schooling in the globalised economy', *Education and Social Justice*, 3 (2): 45–59.

Hill, D. and Cole, M. (2001) *Schooling and Equality: Fact Concept and Policy*, London: Kogan Page.

Jackson, P. W. (1968) *Life in Classrooms*, New York: Holt, Rinehart and Winston.

Kuper, A. (1999) *Culture: The Anthropologists' Account*, Cambridge: Harvard University Press.

Laws, D. (2008) in BBC News (2008) 'White working class boys failing', http://news.bbc.co.uk/1/hi/education/7220683. stm [accessed 12 June 2008].

Meighan, R. and Siraj-Blatchford, I. (2007) *A Sociology of Educating*, 5th edition, London: Continuum.

Murphy, L., Mufti, E. and Kassem, D. (2008, in press) *Education Studies: An Introduction*, Milton Keynes: Oxford University Press.

Phillips, T. (2008) 'Poor white boys are victims too' in the *Sunday Times*, 27 April 2008 www.timesonline.co.uk/tol/ comment/columnists/guest_contributors/article3822685.ece [accessed 28 July 2008].

Reay, D., David, M. and Ball, S. (2005) *Degrees of Choice: Social Class, Race and Gender in Higher Education*, Stoke-on-Trent: Trentham Books.

Steedman, C. (1985) 'The mother made conscious: The historical development of a primary school pedagogy', *History Workshop Journal*, 20 (1): 149–63.

Willis, P. (1977) *Learning to Labour*, Hampshire: Saxon House.

Inclusive education: Where are the gypsies and travellers?

Dean Garratt and Heather Piper

Introduction

This chapter considers the education of gypsy and traveller children[1] and argues that, despite many interventions by successive governments to improve their experience, little obvious progress has been made. Our intentions are twofold: first we point to contradictory policies that impact on the education of gypsies; secondly we draw attention to the wider cultural arena in order to challenge the stereotypes that continue to reinforce the status quo by caricaturing and/or 'romanticizing' gypsy culture. The argument sits within our broader concern to establish a workable agenda for social inclusion. The first half of the chapter draws attention to some historical antecedents and outlines the impact of relevant government policy and legislative change. Some of these changes were intended to assist the plight of gypsies and traveller children; however, the changes having been implemented alongside a different set of legislation (which has led to the reduction of the number of dwelling sites around the country) has meant that very little improvement has been achieved. Gypsy and traveller children continue to be systematically disadvantaged, especially in educational contexts, despite the well-documented imperatives of the United Nations Convention on the Rights of the Child (UNCRC).

The second half of the chapter foregrounds the cultural influences that perpetuate and reinforce stereotypical thinking in relation to gypsy and traveller culture, in a sense repeating the same errors identified in some multicultural and anti-racist teaching, emphasizing difference and creating a 'them' and 'us' scenario (see, for example, Said (1978), for a discussion of the exotic in this regard) rather than problematizing difference in more positive ways. In presenting this argument, we are anxious not to appear to propose to set the pendulum swinging away from the positive action, which characterizes much current anti-racist teaching back towards ignoring discrimination. Instead we are suggesting a move towards the fine (and admittedly elusive) balancing point where difference can be considered in complex, but more useful, ways that recognize that romanticizing and/or hating, for example, are not far apart. Paradoxically gypsies, by being ignored, have been allowed the space for fluidity in and between identities similar to the majority population, yet have simultaneously tended to remain invisible so that their needs have failed to be met. Those outside mainstream education tend to be subdivided into 'the deserving (it is not their fault) and the non-deserving (they bring it on themselves)' (Jordan and Padfield, 2003), and gypsies and travellers clearly fall into the latter group. Ironically, the UK media has also contributed to this (mis)perception, devoting considerable attention to the theme of inclusion, and in particular to the lived experiences of gypsy travellers; the many documentaries and news reports would suggest this is becoming an issue of wider public concern, albeit for conflicting reasons linked to wider social policy (e.g. 'Stamp on a Camp' tabloid campaign spring 2005 and then in spring 2008 a new camp appeared very near to Tessa Joules country cottage).

Policy backdrop

Throughout the 1960s and 1970s, a concerted effort was made to improve the quality of educational support for gypsy traveller children. In 1975, a Schools Council Project noted that urgent action was required to address traveller children's access to, and attendance at school (Reiss, 1975). In response, Local Education Authorities (LEAs) across the UK attempted to create more mobile provision for gypsy travellers, and during the 1980s some 130 LEAs succeeded in doing so. The influence of LEA based traveller education services, in tandem with the later contribution of the European Federation for the Education of Children of Occupational Travellers, led to profound and beneficial change in the way the educational needs of traveller children were identified and managed. Arguably, these changes occurred during a time when the welfare of travellers was relatively low on the list of government priorities, but the combined effort of these agencies led to the development of distance learning materials which were intended to be more relevant to gypsy children. In spite of these efforts, however, provision for the education of gypsies and travellers at the time failed to acknowledge that in mobile communities there is little or no demarcation between social life and work. Home is a family group, not the caravan or any specific place, and family life revolves around work opportunities, with *all* members being involved and included (Okely,

1983; Jordan, 2001). Current provision aimed specifically at children and young people fails to take this connectivity into account. Interestingly, and indicative of the risks of stereotypical categorization, this characteristic of mobile communities where work and leisure are indistinguishable has more in common with so-called middle-class norms. In the past this phenomena was described as an 'extension pattern' where work and leisure overlap, in contrast to a 'neutrality pattern' where there is a clear distinction between the two, as typified for many of those engaged in working-class occupations eager to 'clock off' and get on with real life (Parker, 1972).

The drive to improve educational provision

The drive to improve educational provision for traveller children coincided with the impact of the 1968 Caravan Sites Act. While on paper this Act imposed on local authorities the responsibility to provide sites for gypsy travellers, in practice it was never fully implemented. A principal implication of this lack of commitment was that travellers found it increasingly difficult to settle as they were quickly moved on by local authorities and police. Attempts by LEAs to provide more mobile educational services became an issue of primary importance. However, the Conservative government in the 1980s elected to reduce funding for traveller education, and the Swann Report noted that the underlying consequence of such actions was to exclude gypsies from mainstream education (DES, 1985). In any case, distance learning was originally intended for independent and mature learners rather than those assumed to require additional provision (Jordan, 2001). It is perhaps unsurprising that by the end of the 1980s the vulnerability of traveller students was raised as an issue, especially in relation to their access to secondary education (Hyman, 1989).

Useful Websites

Gypsy traveller A website that supports individuals working with gypsy and traveller children	www.gypsy-traveller.org/cyberpilots/adult_section/new_professional.htm
Research into the education of gypsy traveller children in Wales NFER website gypsy education	www.nfer.ac.uk/research-areas/pims-data/summaries/research-into-the-education-of-gypsy-traveller-children-in-wales.cfm
Travellers and literacy Literacy trust website with articles on gypsy and traveller literacy	www.literacytrust.org.uk/database/travellers.html
Gypsy Roma traveller General website for gypsy and traveller communities	www.grthm.co.uk/

The introduction of the Criminal Justice and Public Order Act 1994 (which superseded the 1968 Act), gave police the power (under section 61) to direct trespassers to leave private land where: 'The landowner has taken action to request that the trespassers leave and they do not do so; there are six or more vehicles on the land; or damage has been caused to the land, or there has been abusive, threatening or insulting behaviour by the trespassers.' The police also have powers (under section 62) to seize and impound the vehicles of travelling people, who are directed to leave land and do not do so in reasonable time. A disproportionate use of this power would violate Article 1 of the First Protocol to the European Convention on Human Rights as well as Articles 8 and 14, but evidence suggests that the police rarely use all the legal means at their disposal, although they may threaten to do so.

Local authorities and travellers

In effect the 1994 Act removed the responsibility from local authorities to provide sites for travellers, and this has resulted in transforming nomadic culture into a form of criminal activity, viewed by some as 'genocidal in effect' (McVeigh, 1997). One in five travellers now has no legal or secure place to stay (DfES, 2003), and this lived reality has affected gypsy communities in a variety of ways (Kiddle, 1999), including gypsies purchasing land which in turn has led to difficulties with planning authorities, etc. The 1994 Act can be interpreted as having undermined the positive intentions of LEAs and the then Department for Education and Employment (DfEE)/Department for Education and Skills (DfES) in enabling gypsy children wider access to full-time education. Indeed, in some cases there has been 'growing resistance in schools to the admission of traveller children' (Currie and Danaher, 2001: 35). A narrowly defined academic curriculum and preoccupation with performance league tables has made present institutional arrangements and imperatives unpalatable and largely oppositional to the educational and cultural needs of gypsy travellers. Meanwhile, gypsies are technically protected by Race Relations legislation, but are nonetheless subjected to various types of legal and institutional racism (Derrington and Kendal, 2004). In any case, being protected by Race Relations legislation requires being accepted as a race in the first place, yet 'successive governments have been able to avoid offering them (gypsies and travellers) the protection afforded to other minorities by refusing to recognize them as an ethnic minority but rather a group who masquerades as such' (Carter, 2002: 12–13). This situation has resonance with issues raised in the Macpherson Report, in particular the articulation of institutional racism which is expressed thus:

> The collective failure of an organisation to provide an appropriate and professional service to people because of their colour, culture, or ethnic origin. It can be detected in processes, attitudes and behaviour which amount to discrimination through unwitting prejudice, ignorance, thoughtlessness and racist stereotyping which disadvantage minority ethnic people. It persists because of the failure of the organisation openly and adequately to recognise and address its existence

and causes by policy, example and leadership. Without recognition and action to eliminate such racism, it can prevail as part of the ethos or culture of the organisation. It is a corrosive disease.
(Macpherson, 1999: para. 6.34)

Institutional racism

The view that institutional racism is manifest in policy which is in effect culturally biased, has led Currie and Danaher to argue that there is an inherent 'mismatch in recent government policy which in its pursuit of school improvement actually contradicts and hinders its laudable but increasingly sidelined social inclusion policy' (2001: 33). For example, travellers in Scotland of secondary schooling age have reported difficulties in satisfying the requirements of the curriculum, as the development of an assessment portfolio has proved incompatible with a mobile lifestyle, prompting drop-out (Jordan, 2001). But for gypsies, institutional racism is only part of the picture. Others (Kenrick and Clarke, 1999) have cited examples of prejudice and negative attitudes among parents in relation to gypsy children who are integrated in mainstream classrooms. In a survey by the Citizen Traveller Campaign, one thousand settled Irish adults were asked about their attitude towards the inclusion of thirteen different minority groups. Travellers came second from bottom, just above drug addicts and 70 per cent of respondents said they would not accept a traveller as a friend (reported by Birkett (2002)).

Forty years after the Plowden Report documented that young gypsies were the 'most severely deprived children in the country' (DES, 1967), little has changed regarding their inclusion within formal education (Reiss, 1975; HMI, 1983; Hyman, 1989; Ofsted, 1996; Wood, 1997); their legal rights to security (DfES, 2003); and repeated exposure to racial discrimination, institutional and personal (DES, 1985; Bhopal, 2000; Derrington and Kendall, 2004). Given this context, it is hardly surprising that recent estimates suggest only 15–20 per cent of traveller children are enrolled at schools (Ofsted, 1996; CRE, 2007), and similar attitudes towards young gypsies are in evidence elsewhere across Europe (Liegois, 1998). Chomsky reminds us that gypsies remain excluded in all the countries where they live, and claims nobody gives a damn about the gypsies (Chomsky, 1994). Evidence to support this assessment would include the following quote from an elected legislator:

They are scum, and I use the word advisedly. People who do what these people have done do not deserve the same human rights as my decent constituents going about their everyday lives.
(National Children's Bureau, 2005)

Current initiatives

The most recent government attempts at alleviating some of the difficulties include the production of guidelines: Aiming High: Raising the Achievement of Gypsy and Traveller Pupils: A Guide to Good Practice (DfES, 2003). This guide, as the title suggests, is concerned with the development of effective policies and practices to help raise the achievement of gypsy and traveller pupils. From 2003, for the first time, gypsy/Roma and travellers of Irish Heritage pupils (the two largest groups within the UK gypsy and traveller communities) were included in the Pupil Level Annual School Census (PLASC) data, as categories in their own right. Scotland has produced separate documentation: Taking a closer look at Inclusion and Equality – meeting the need of gypsies and travellers complements another document: Partnership with a route to quality and fairness (HMIE, 2005). In addition to the above guidelines, under the Race Relations (Amendment) Act 2000, it is now necessary for schools to monitor and assess the impact of their policies on children from gypsy/Roma and travellers of Irish Heritage communities.

Funding issues

Schools in England and Wales currently receive the same funding for gypsy and traveller children as they do for all children on the school roll through the Education Formula Spending Share (but gypsy children need to be on roll on the annual census day to qualify). However, in addition gypsy and traveller children also attract the Vulnerable Children's Grant (VCG). From April 2003 the VCG merged several Standards' Fund Grants, including the Traveller Achievement Grant and made available 84 million pounds (in comparison with 31 million pounds in 2002), which has since remained more or less static. The VCG allows Local Authorities to allocate funding based on local needs so as to provide support to a range of vulnerable children, including those from gypsy and traveller backgrounds. Funding for gypsy and traveller children from this source mainly goes to the Traveller Education Support Services. According to *Hansard* (19 January 2004, column WA124) Baroness Ashton of Upholland informed her Lordships that: 'the department is additionally funding a project in six LEAs at secondary school level which aims to improve attendance, raise attainment and engage gypsy/traveller parents through encouraging best practice.' In spite of such initiative and good intentions, we would argue that, given the weight of the contradictory legislation, it seems prudent to remain sceptical as to whether such funding is likely to bring about positive outcomes for young gypsies.

Extent of discrimination

The seriousness and scale of this problem continues despite the adoption of the UNCRC, ratified by 192 states across the globe. Such rights are intended as a safeguard against the abuse of state power, but it can be argued that successive UK (and other) governments have continued to discriminate against travellers in ways that are potentially damaging to the educational entitlement of young gypsies. This point is even more sensitive given the fact that historically (and in terms of citizenship education) children have been seen as 'not yets...not yet knowing, not yet competent, and not yet being' (Verhellen, 2000: 33), implying they are not quite ready to engage with the moral challenge or 'real business' of education. This is antithetical to the 'traditional' pattern of interactions within some gypsy communities where, for example, young children are included in adult conversation and in work domains, and where they are expected to become useful contributing members of their extended family and community (Jordan, 2001). With this cultural context in mind, it would seem that young gypsies are being further disadvantaged by mainstream society which claims to be promoting the rights of children, but actually inadvertently marginalizes them.

Such consequences are in contrast with Article 28 of the UNCRC, which is unequivocal in stating that all children have the right to free education. In addition, Article 29 contains detailed provisions concerning 'the development of the child's personality to its fullest potential; the preparation of the child for a responsible role in society; the development of respect for nature; mutual understanding and friendship among all peoples; and especially the development of respect for human rights and fundamental freedoms' (Verhellen, 2000: 39). Arguably, this is precisely what occurs within certain gypsy lifestyles, without any intrusion of formal educational policy. So while in the Citizenship Order it is suggested that young people should be provided with opportunities to develop understanding of their obligations to society (QCA, 1999) the process by which this is promoted has the very opposite effect for some gypsy children. Of course, this suggests that beyond the child's legal right to education there are further rights *in* education, which embrace important political and social dimensions which through formal or informal means encourage the development of critically informed views. This ambition is underpinned by Articles 12–16 of the UNCRC, which articulates important fundamental freedoms, including the freedom to express opinion, freedom of thought, freedom of conscience and religion, and freedom of association (Verhellen, 2000). Such freedoms are crucial for traveller children who may be excluded by the pervasive influence of the social and cultural forces that permeate mainstream education. However, while the UK government could do much to alleviate this problem, it would be too simplistic an argument to suggest this issue is exclusively a state responsibility or that a move towards wider participation would provide a cure for all the educational difficulties experienced by young gypsies.

Activity

Make notes on the following questions:

1. Are gypsy and travelling communities the greatest challenge to the notion of social inclusion, fully highlighting the tensions around multiculturalism and integration?
2. Are there any other ethnic minority groups in a similar situation? If so, who and how?

Cultural influences

In this second half of the chapter we position the education of gypsy and traveller children in a wider cultural arena, in order to take issue with the stereotypes that continue to be associated with young gypsies, especially those who are typified as educational problems and as a result often excluded for extended periods from secondary education (Archer and Yamashita, 2003). Clearly, it can be argued that some of the problems facing gypsies and travellers have resulted from much broader economic, social and cultural changes than cannot solely be attributed to UK policy and legislation. Therefore debates about gypsy identity, culture and traditions, are necessarily rehearsed against the wider canvas of globalization and the attendant imperatives to encourage growth in international trade as well as social and geographical mobility. Nayek (2003: 147), for example, suggests that 'emerging post-industrial masculinities cannot be fully understood through micro-institutional approaches that make school the sole focus of inquiry [but] must be situated in the intersecting pathways of family biography, history, locality and global transformations'. Within the UK (and elsewhere) such trends have led to interaction and integration of European national economic systems, through cross-border investment, and capital flows (Giddens, 1998). Changes in the constitution of European society (including the progressive development of the EU) have helped to create fertile and supportive conditions for new alliances. However, some of these changes have had unintended consequences and have assisted the creation of tensions, patterns of exclusion, and notions of belonging and disenfranchisement, through the creation of 'in groups' and 'out groups'. This is not a new phenomenon; the UK has long been characterized by migrations, population inflows and outflows, which have usually accompanied times of political and social change, and in retrospect these tend to be regarded in a positive light. But when it comes to gypsies, it has been argued that their 'identity' has become 'split' or hybridized and that their 'cultural histories…[are increasingly]…distinguished by discontinuity, differences, and social displacement' (Levinson and Sparkes, 2004: 707). The implication of such an account is that any hybridity of identity of gypsies is a bad thing. On the face of it this would appear to be a positive statement of support for the continuation of strong traditional gypsy lifestyles. Yet such statements inadvertently fall into the trap of assuming gypsies are different to the rest of 'us' (who are more free to choose lifestyles and identities for ourselves); and also could be taken as assuming the importance of purity of gypsy blood-lines that need protecting and preserving, which from one interpretation is (presumably unwittingly) racist.

Impetus to a nomadic lifestyle

Alongside hybridization (for which read reproducing with an 'out-group' member), some have argued that gypsies feel they have lost their 'homeland' by effectively being forced to give up their nomadic lifestyles (Levinson and Sparkes, 2004). As a consequence they have become disunited, or simply become part of a 'vanished folk culture' (Sibley, 1981: 18). Others have seen beyond this, arguing instead that the traditions live on because the 'significance of place is embedded in the narrative that circulates among groups', and thus they remain intrinsic to gypsies' sense of cultural identity regardless of wherever they may happen to be living (Bird, 2002, cited in Levinson and Sparkes, 2004: 707). It is perhaps worth remembering that the nomadic condition is not an immutable cultural feature *per se*, but was the result of challenging social conditions and the fear and need to flee from prosecutions and expulsions (Machiels, 2002). Others (Carter, 2002) have pointed out that accounts of gypsy culture tend to follow one of two stereotypes: the criminalized and dangerous *or* the romanticized and nomadic (the latter often being more apparent in art and literature than in the actual lived experience of many gypsies). Stories of a nomadic lifestyle clearly follow the romanticized tradition whether told by gypsies or others speaking for/about them, for example: 'it seems that the concept of nomadism can survive the apparent demise of the reality' (Levinson and Sparkes, 2004: 707). However, nostalgic hankering after a romantic past or golden age is not only pertinent to gypsies. It is also common in discussion around multiculturalism and integration, and is present in most societies' rehearsed tales of the past.

Reality

In reality, gypsies and travellers are a disparate and culturally entangled (Archer and Yamashita, 2003) group just like other social groups, whether they are fully nomadic, static, or only periodically settled. What is important here are the significant cultural influences that have led to their non-participation in formal schooling in general, and secondary education in particular; their non-participation being much higher than for any other group. It is claimed that within gypsy societies there is a widespread mistrust of 'mainstream' culture and a growing conviction that the impact of *gauje*/mainstream education can be harmful, influencing young gypsies in largely undesirable ways. Gypsy and traveller children appear more able to benefit from the content and utility of primary education (in terms of equipping them with important life skills like reading and writing) but by the age of secondary schooling it is reported that education is regarded as being potentially damaging and/or increasingly irrelevant. Whatever else these circulating discourses may reveal, using language such as 'potentially damaging' suggests fear on the part of some gypsies. While many may view secondary education to be irrelevant to their lifestyles (as do many other young people), such views also result from being made unwelcome and from the experience of racial bullying (Derrington and Kendall, 2004).

Conflict of value systems

Our contention is that the conflicting value systems that arise from living in two parallel cultural worlds (Derrington and Kendall, 2004), have been sustained by the creation of oppositional discourses. Cultural dissonance is a product of perceptions of group difference, invoked by social boundaries between sections of the population, creating a culture of 'us' and 'them' that progressively becomes more deeply entrenched. Hancock (2000), for example, has argued that too much emphasis on formal learning is considered threatening to the Romany way of life. The longer the periods for which travellers are based in school, the greater the likelihood they will yield to the influences of the majority culture. It is argued that gypsy children become increasingly disenchanted at school after the onset of adolescence: a time when behavioural expectations within school become increasingly ill matched with established roles at home (Levinson and Sparkes, 2003). We have already suggested one explanation for this so-called ill match, although these issues become more acute at the level of secondary education, where opportunities to mix with members of the opposite sex and with non-traveller peers present numerous temptations. It is claimed that many gypsies are anxious that their children will be lured away from nomadism and become 'normalized' by mainstream society (Clay, 1999). However, it is hard to see how these claims are pertinent only to gypsies and travellers, and indeed members of religious groups (and others) could be said to be at least as concerned about adolescent sexuality, and the irrelevance of secondary education has continued to remain a problem for many working-class young people – hence the recourse to the ubiquitous categories 'disaffected' and 'disengaged' (DfEE, 1997a, 1997b).

Gypsy culture as a romanticized commodity

Indeed, these arguments tend to assume that gypsy culture exists 'out there' as a romanticized commodity, capable of being rescued and restored, and protected from all unwarranted intrusions. It is perhaps not surprising that many gypsies feel threatened by the values of mainstream education/society, or that they have tended to stereotype *gauje* education as 'oppositional' or 'irrelevant' (Hancock, 2000), particularly as gypsies have reaped fewer of the rewards of economic success (unemployment is at an all time high for gypsies and travellers). It is easy to see how secondary education with its 'enlightened', liberative, equality-based values represents a discourse that is wholly oppositional (Clay, 1999). However, the separateness of the gypsy and traveller community makes such dissonance more explicit and potentially stressful, which may explain why some young gypsies choose to attempt to hide (pass) their real identities in order to gain acceptance from others (Acton, 1974; Tajfel, 1978; Lee, 1993; Hancock, 1997; NCB, 2005). This phenomenon deserves further, serious interrogation.

Strategies for identity

One identified coping strategy adopted by some members of the perceived embattled gypsy culture is associated with language traditions. It is argued that these are employed to create and maintain boundaries between traveller communities and mainstream society. English gypsy travellers, for example, retain the use of Anglo-Romani (a mixture of English (80 per cent) and Romani (20 per cent)) so they are able to switch codes in order to make themselves unintelligible to outsiders. Courthiade (1993) has suggested that even for those who do not speak Anglo-Romani, the language remains a significant cultural reference point which affirms the shared identity of gypsy communities while simultaneously creating distance between themselves and mainstream society (though we recognize this is by no means unique to gypsy culture, and may also be illustrated, for example, by the use of Welsh in the presence of English-speaking incomers, or of Yiddish in East London in the 1950s and 1960s). For traveller children, the ability to switch linguistic codes confers a special status that is valued within their community. It can also be usefully employed as a device to exclude non-traveller children or, alternatively, utilized as a source of pride where bilingual talents can be used to gain acceptance with non-travellers (Derrington and Kendall, 2004).

Catalyst for change

It seems likely that factors which also applied within the majority population at varying points in history may operate as a catalyst for change within gypsy culture. While the influence of globalization across Europe, and the reduction of dwelling sites within the UK can mean that gypsies are increasingly difficult to reach, more permeable European boundaries provide the preconditions where gypsy identities are simultaneously fractured, hybridized *and* united across borders. Mobile phones must have had an effect in this regard, and the internet could also prove significant. Tensions within policies, practices and government legislation, generate the potential for points of resistance, and hence the freedom that creates further possibilities for change in the future. The reality is complex, and unhelpful stereotypes should be replaced by educational approaches that reflect and seek to address such complexity.

Activity

Answer the following question:

1. Does the case of gypsy and traveller children show that there is an intrinsic contradiction between prioritizing school improvements and targets while also expecting schools to serve as engines of social inclusion?

Conclusion

Throughout this chapter we have drawn attention to the implications of policy and practice that impact negatively on the lives on many young (and other) gypsies. Given the history and weight of contradictory legislation, it is likely that change will not come easily. If educationalists remain uncritical in their stance and continue to convey stereotypical views of gypsy society (i.e. as either romantic or dangerous), then arguably the task of reform is made even more difficult. In our view, future policy needs to reflect a more critical understanding of the nuances and complexities inherent in gypsy culture, just as the subtleties of mainstream groups have been considered, including the recognition that all 'groups' are not discrete, and that 'going native' is part and parcel of a multicultural society. There is no blueprint that is likely to succeed for the education of all gypsies, anymore than there is a blueprint that will work for all members of 'mainstream' society. The inherent problem lies in the 'fixing' of a cultural stereotype which caricatures the social category and in reality is part of the problem rather than contributing to the solution. If education can assist young people to be more critical in their approach to these and similar issues, this will surely lead to better research and more effective policy making in the future. Currently, while the rhetoric of UK 'Citizenship' (QCA, 1999) might include gypsies and travellers – lived experiences appear to be very different.

Key Points

- Interventions by government to raise educational attainment for gypsy and traveller children have consistently failed
- The main reason for the failure to raise educational achievement is contained in the contradictory policies pursued in relation to the gypsy traveller community
- One of the key issues is the failure to recognize the disparate nature of the gypsy traveller community
- In the 1960s and 1970s provision was made for gypsy and traveller communities through the requirement that local authorities should provide sites for the community
- The 1990s saw a change in the law and local authorities were relieved of the legal duty to provide sites for nomadic communities to settle
- In terms of education there has been a general failure to recognize the needs of gypsy and traveller children
- The lack of education for gypsy and traveller children is in direct conflict with the UN convention on the Rights of the Child
- The educational, social care and legal structures in society are constituted in such as way as to exhibit institutional discrimination against gypsy and traveller communities – as defined by the Macpherson Report on the murder of Stephen Lawrence
- There have been attempts to raise levels of educational achievement under the New Labour government – (through such policies as: Aiming High), this includes trying to increase school attendance but by and large these have failed
- Issues of identity and recognition of community needs are not taken into account
- When educational provision is successful it is at the primary rather than secondary phase – with the onset of adolescence there is a feeling that contact with the wider community is irrelevant to gypsy traveller needs
- Gypsy traveller communities are effectively excluded from wider society, not only in the UK but across Europe – they constitute the 'other' or outsider.

Further Reading

David Gillborn (2008) *Racism and Education Coincidence or Conspiracy?*, London: Routledge.

Kenrick, D. and Clarke, C. (1999) *Moving On: The Gypsies and Travellers of Britain*, Hatfield: University of Hertfordshire Press.

Kiddle, C. (1999) *Traveller Children: A Voice for Themselves*, London: Jessica Kingsley.

Note

1. Throughout this chapter we refer to gypsies and travellers interchangeably. While we are aware of important key distinctions, for the purpose of this chapter (and for brevity) we conflate these categories in order to promote our argument for inclusion which applies equally to all groups.

References

Acton, T. A. (1974) *Gypsy Politics and Social Change*, London: Routledge and Kegan Paul.

Archer, L. and Yamashita, H. (2003) *Theorising Inner-City Masculinities: 'Race', Class, Gender and Education*, 15 (2): 115–32.

Bhopal, K. with Gundara, J., Jones, C. and Owen, C. (2000) *Working towards Inclusive Education for Gypsy Traveller Pupils* (RR 238), London: DfEE.

Bird, S. (2002) 'It makes sense to us: Cultural identity in local legends of place', *Journal of Contemporary Ethnography*, 31 (5): 519–47.

Birkett, D. (2002) 'School for scandal', *Guardian*, 15 January: 12.

Carter, H. (2002) 'Race, romanticism and perspectives on gypsy education in early twentieth century Britain', *Journal of Contemporary History*, 5.

Chomsky, N. (1994) *Keeping the Rabble in Line: Interviews with David Barsamian*, Edinburgh: AK Press.

Clay, S. (1999) 'Traveller Children's Schooling', Cardiff, University of Wales: Unpublished doctoral thesis.

Commission for race equality (CRE) (2007) *Home Page*, www.cre.gov.uk [accessed 7 Mar. 2007].

Courthiade, M. (1993) 'The work of research and action groups on Romani linguistics', *Interface*, 9: 3–7.

Currie, H. and Danaher, P. H. (2001) 'Government funding for English travellers education support services', *Multicultural Teaching*, 19 (2), Spring edition.

Department of Education and Science (DES) (1967) *Children and Their Primary Schools. The Plowden Report. Central Advisory Council for Education (England)*, London: HMSO.

Department of Education and Science (DES) (1985) *Education for All: The Report of the Committee of Enquiry into the Education of Children from Ethnic Minority Groups (The Swann Report)*, London: HMSO.

Department for Education and Employment (DfEE) (1997a) *Directory of Careers Service Work with Disaffected Young People*, London: HMSO.

Department for Education and Employment (DfEE) (1997b) *Survey of Careers Service Work with Disaffected Young People*, London: HMSO.

Department for Education and Skills (DfES) (2003) *Aiming High: Raising Achievement of Minority Ethnic Pupils*, London: DfES.

Derrington, C. and Kendall, S. (2004) *Gypsy Traveller Students in Secondary Schools – Culture, Identity and Achievement*, Stoke-on-Trent: Trentham Books.

Giddens, A. (1998) *Third Way – Renewal of Social Democracy*, Oxford: Blackwell.

Hancock, I. (1997) 'The struggle for the control of identity', *Patrin Web Journal*, 4, 4.

Hancock, I. (2000) 'Standardisation and ethnic defence in emergent non-literate societies: the gypsy and Caribbean cases', in T. Acton and M. Dalphinis (eds), *Language, Blacks and Gypsies*, London: Whiting and Birch Ltd.

Her Majesty's Inspectorate (HMI) (1983) *The Education of Travellers' Children*, London: HMSO.

Her Majesty's Inspectorate in Education (HMIE) (2005) *Taking a Closer Look at Inclusion and Equality – Meeting the Need of Gypsies and Travellers*, Astron B39203, February 2005.

Hyman, M. (1989) *Sites for Travellers*, London: Runnymede Trust.

Jordan, E. (2001) 'From interdependence, to dependence and independence; home and school learning for Traveller children', *Childhood: A Global Journal of Child Research*, 8 (1): 57–74.

Jordan, E. and Padfield, P. (2003) 'Education at the margins: outsiders and the mainstream, in T. G. K. Bryce and W. M. Humes (eds), *Scottish Education: Post-Devolution*, 2nd edition, Edinburgh: Edinburgh University Press.

Kenrick, D. and Clarke, C. (1999) *Moving On: The Gypsies and Travellers of Britain*, Hatfield: University of Hertfordshire Press.

Kiddle, C. (1999) *Traveller Children: A Voice for Themselves*, London: Jessica Kingsley.

Lee, N. (1993) 'Gypsies and travellers in the United Kingdom', *The Education of Gypsy and Traveller Children*, Report of European Conference in 1989, ACERT.

Levinson, M. P. and Sparkes, A. C. (2003) 'Gypsy masculinities and the school-home interface: exploring contradictions and tensions', *British Journal of Sociology of Education*, 24 (5): 587–603.

Levinson, M. P. and Sparkes, A. C. (2004) 'Gypsy identity and orientations to space', *Journal of Contemporary Ethnography*, 33 (6): 704–34.

Liegois, J-P. (1998) *School Provision for Ethnic Minorities – The Gypsy Paradigm*, 2nd edition, Hatfield: University of Hertfordshire Press.

Machiels, T. (2002) *Keeping the Distance or Taking the Chances. Roma and Travellers in Western Europe*, Brussels: ENAR.

Macpherson, W. (1999) *The Stephen Lawrence Inquiry*, London: The Stationery Office.

McVeigh, R. (1997) 'Theorising sedentarism: the roots of anti-nomadism', in T. Acton (ed.), *Gypsy Politics and Traveller Identity*, Hatfield: University of Hertfordshire Press.

National Children's Bureau (2005) *Gypsy and Traveller Children*, Highlight no. 221, London: NCB.

Nayek, A (2003) 'Boyz to men; masculinities, schooling and labour transitions in de-industrial times', *Educational Review*, 55 (2): 147–59.

Office for Standards in Education (Ofsted) (1996) *The Education of Travelling Children*, London: Ofsted.

Okely, J. (1983) *The Traveller-Gypsies*, Cambridge: Cambridge University Press.

Parker, S. R. (1972) *The Future of Work and Leisure*, London: Paladin.

Qualification and Curriculum Authority (QCA) (1999) *Citizenship*, London: QCA.

Reiss, C. (1975) *Education of Travelling Children*, London: Macmillan.

Said, E. (1978) *Orientalism*, London: Routledge and Kegan Paul.

Sibley, D. (1981) *Outsiders in Urban Societies*, Oxford: Basil Blackwell.

Tajfel, H. (1978) *The Social Psychology of Minorities*, London: Minority Rights Group.

Verhellen, E. (2000) 'Children's rights and education', in A. Osler (ed.), *Citizenship and Democracy in Schools: Diversity, Identity, Equality*, Stoke-on-Trent: Trentham Books.

Wood, M. (1997) 'Home-school work with traveller children and their families', in J. Bastiani (ed.), *Home-School Work in Multicultural Settings*, London: David Fulton.

Inner-city education

John Robinson and Marilyn Eccles

Introduction

One of the distinguishing features of education in the inner cities in the UK, and elsewhere, is not the disparities between the highest and lowest achievers nor the gap between the advantaged and the disadvantaged, but rather the degree of concentration of these disparities. Differences exist in the cities, in the suburbs, in towns and in rural communities. However, in the inner cities these differences tend to be hyperconcentrated and so give rise to a density of disadvantage that raises particular issues for educators and learners in the inner cities. In this chapter, we are going to explore these hyperconcentrated disparities. We will then consider the policy responses by the current New Labour government to these inequities. After setting out these issues, we will examine how these inequities give rise to five contradictions in educational experiences of learners in the inner cities: contradictions of power; contradictions of class; contradictions of gender; contradictions of ethnicity; and contradictions of literacy.

The inequities of inner-city education

In addressing issues relating to inner-city education, it is evident that there are significant inequalities in access to and outcomes of access to educational resources. In order to illustrate this, we provide a picture of one large English conurbation as a backdrop to the discussion that follows. In Greater Manchester 425,950 children and young people attend 1,288 schools and 23 colleges. There is a wide range of ethnic communities with a higher than national average representation of black and minority ethnic (BME) children and young people, particularly Asian heritage children and young people. Approximately 16 per cent of the learners have a first-language other than English. Around 20.4 per cent are eligible for free school meals (FSM). Only 92 of the 1,288 schools are considered to be outstanding by Ofsted, with 43 schools having a Notice to Improve or requiring special measures. Forty-three of the schools fall below the Government target of 30 per cent of learners achieving five A*–C grades at GCSE including English and mathematics. At Key Stage 2 attainment in core subjects is in line with national averages, however, by Key Stage 3 they have fallen behind in terms of attainment and progression and this continues in to Key Stage 4. The average absence rate in Secondary Schools is 8.1 per cent compared with 7.9 per cent nationally. Of those who have left school 8.1 per cent of the age cohort is not in employment, education or training (NEETS) compared with 6.6 per cent nationally (DCSF, 2008: 12).

Useful Websites

Search Institute
Search Institute is a leading global innovator in discovering what children and adolescents need to become caring, healthy, and responsible adults.

www.search-institute.org/

EiC – standards site
The official government site for
Excellence in the Cities

www.standards.dfes.gov.uk/sie/eic/

Joseph Rowntree Foundation
An organization that funds research into poverty and community issues

www.jrf.org.uk/

The Poverty site
A website that provides research and statistics on poverty in the UK

www.poverty.org.uk/summary/
rural%20 intro.shtml

Child Poverty Action Group
A non-governmental organization that campaigns on issues relating to child poverty

www.cpag.org.uk/

Location of deficits

Mostly, these deficits are concentrated in the inner-city areas of the conurbation. These are not just statistics – they depict real people's lives and illustrate that inequities really matter. For example, in a sample of 12,000 children, by the age of 3, children from disadvantaged families are already lagging a full year behind their middle-class contemporaries in understanding colours, letters, shapes and sizes and 10 months behind in vocabulary tests (Carvel, 2007, Institute of Education, 2007). In addition, only 14 per cent of variation in individuals' performance is accounted for by school quality. Most variation is explained by reference to other factors including the lives of children and young people inside and outside school (Hirsch, 2007). In explaining differences in achievement at GCSE, the most significant explanatory factor in terms of statistically relevant causality is postcode (Walters, 2007).

Enduring inequalities

These inequalities appear to be obdurate and enduring. The Sutton Trust reports that when considering relationships between intermediate outcomes (degree attainment, test scores and non-cognitive abilities) and parental income for cohorts born between 1970 and 2000 there is no evidence that these relationships have changed over this period and that parental background continues to exert a very significant influence on the academic progress of children:

> [t]hose from the poorest fifth of households but in the brightest group at age three drop from the 88th percentile on cognitive tests at age three to the 65th percentile at age five. Those from the richest households who are least able at age three move up from the 15th percentile to the 45th percentile by age five. If this trend were to continue, the children from affluent backgrounds who are doing poorly at age three would be likely to overtake the poorer but initially bright children in test scores by age seven. Inequalities in degree acquisition meanwhile persist across different income groups. While 44 per cent of young people from the richest 20 per cent of households acquired a degree in 2002, only 10 per cent from the poorest 20 per cent of households did so. The UK remains low in the international rankings of social mobility when compared with other advanced nations. (Blanden and Machin, 2007: 1)

The correlation between underachievement and social disadvantage

There is a strong correlation between social and economic disadvantage and educational achievement. Approximately 70 per cent of the most deprived areas in the UK are found in the four cities of Glasgow, London, Liverpool and Manchester. They are home to 128 of the top 128 wards where more than half of families are out of work and relying on benefits. Many of these families experience life at or below the poverty line. Families living in poverty are a high predictor of poor educational outcomes for young people living in such families. Raffo (2006) reports that the Social Exclusion Unit (SEU, 1998) found that five times as many secondary schools in 'worst neighbourhoods' had 'serious weaknesses' (as defined by Ofsted) than was typically the case, and children drawn from poorer family origins were more likely to have been in the lowest quartile of attainment in educational tests compared to their counterparts in other quartiles. Evidence from England shows that, at Key Stage 3, for schools with more than 40 per cent FSM no pupils achieved the standardized age-related performance level in English, compared with 83 per cent of pupils in schools with less than 5 per cent FSM (Raffo, 2006). Raffo (2006) also reports that evidence from the Office of the Deputy Prime Minister in 2005 showed that key attainment in 2001/2 increases steadily from pupils in schools that are located in the most deprived wards to those in schools in the most prosperous wards. The link between poor education outcomes and poverty is predominately an inner-city problem (Raffo, 2006).

Recent government initiatives

Recent policy responses to the concerns raised by these disparities have included Excellence in Cities, Primary Excellence in Cities, Excellence Clusters, the National Literacy and Numeracy Strategy (now the National Primary Strategy), the Key Stage 3 Strategy and Aim Higher. The most recent policy disparities have been the development of the City Challenge Programme. This was initially launched in Greater London in 2003 and from 2008 will include Greater Manchester and the Black Country. This programme is aimed at raising aspirations and educational standards and achievements in 47 local government boroughs (33 in Greater London, 10 in Greater Manchester and 4 in the Black Country) in order to narrow the gap between disadvantaged children and young people and their more successful peers by increasing access to high-quality education. Between 2008 and 2011 the projected budget is 160 million pounds. This programme will involve school leadership development and whole school development with targeted support for schools in challenging circumstances. There is a particular focus on raising the achievements levels of young gifted and talented learners, which aims to increase the take-up rate of university places by disadvantaged but able learners. At the time of writing, it is too early to say whether there have been any significant gains through the programme. However, the launch document for the London Challenge set a very challenging target when it reported that 'pupils from African Caribbean and some Asian background achieve significantly poorer results than average' (DfES, 2003: 27), and accepted that 'only when...Black Caribbean pupils achieve well, can the London Challenge be said to have succeeded' (ibid.: 26). It is difficult to be overly optimistic about this challenge.

Activity

1. What do you think the differences are between inner-city areas and suburban districts in terms of the following:
   - Education
   - Wealth
   - The environment
   - Employment opportunities.
2. Explain how they might impact on an individual's life chances, displaying your ideas in a poster.

The contradictions of inner-city education[1]

Inner-city education is characterized by five main contradictions.

Contradictions of power

According to Castells (1977: 243) 'it is politics which structures the totality of (urban phenomena, including inner-city education) and determines how it is transformed'. By politics, Castells was referring to power struggles between different members of urban communities and between urban communities and local and national governments. An understanding of the politics of inner-city education is crucial for understanding the inequalities we have outlined above. As Grace (2006) comments, there is no simple concept of learning – it is always learning in a given political context. Merson and Campbell (1974) argued that the defining characteristic of inner-city residents is their relative powerlessness. Thus inner-city contexts demonstrate one of their major contradictions – the juxtaposition of power centres and power holders in the political realm, with inner-city communities lacking in political clout and leverage upon policy. In Britain, disillusionment with the formal political process has resulted in growing levels of voter 'apathy' or abstention. Many inner-city residents do not believe that political parties have any sustained programmes for the improvement of their communities and, as a consequence, they do not participate in elections. This compounds the problem, as Galbraith (1992) has noted. If the urban poor are not an active voting constituency, political parties will adjust their programmes in the interest of those who are. Galbraith (1992) also argues that there is a growing influence of 'the political economy of contentment'. This means that the comfortable and contented majority of active voters ('Middle England?') are increasingly embracing a culture of relative private interest. The result of this is that action for the improvement of the inner city and its schools is subject only to short-term interventions rather than to sustained programmes for transformation (Grace, 2006). As Grace notes:

> [i]n a political culture of relative public good, a significant sector of citizens accept the legitimacy of political action taken in support of disadvantaged citizens as a practical expression of commitment to ideas of social justice, equality of opportunity and equity in society. In a political culture of relative private interest a growing number of citizens reject the legitimacy of action in support of the disadvantaged (who are seen to be responsible for their own problems) and support policies designed to enhance their own interests. (1994: 53)

Galbraith (1992) argued that this changed political culture is now very visible in the US and, it can be argued, is developing in Britain too. The social consequences of these developments will be a sharper polarization between the comfortable suburbs and the impoverished inner cities. Urban schools are necessarily caught up in these contradictions of power and locality.

Contradictions of class

For Castells (1977), the contradictions of a class society are expressed concretely in metropolitan cities in the process of formation of residential space and of housing zones.

> By urban segregation, one means the tendency to organize space into zones with a high internal social homogeneity...the distribution of housing produces its social differentiation...since the characteristics of the dwellings and of their residents are at the root of the type and level of amenities and functions that are attached to them. (169)

One of the contradictions arising from this in inner-city schooling is the existence of relative proximity of schools which serve different class and ethnic populations and which have very different success or failure profiles. In other words, in the absence of a city-wide authority having power to regulate school admissions, the tendency in a class-marked city is to reproduce class-marked schools. This leads to the disproportionate representation of socially advantaged children in the most successful schools and of socially disadvantaged children in those schools identified as failing (Whitty, 2002: 84) as a result of enhanced parental choice, increased school autonomy and the free operation of market forces in education. It is in the schools of the urban working class that these processes of social and cultural polarization inevitably produce the 'sink' or failing school that has become overwhelmed by the concentration of challenges that it faces.

Activity

Most educational initiatives by governments seem to concentrate on issues relating to gender and ethnicity – why do you think they tend to ignore class?

Do you think that the education system reinforces class differences in educational attainments or attempts to overcome them? Explain and justify your ideas on these issues to a friend.

Contradictions of gender

One of the contradictions of gender in urban schooling is the widespread belief that girls are now achieving educational 'success' while at the same time evidence shows that this is not the case for many girls in the urban context. Diane Reay points out that

> despite the noisy babble of educational innovation and 'the gender revolution in education', social class relations...are still characterized as much by continuity as by change (and) the resounding educational success of girls spoken of in recent years is primarily about middle-class girls. (2003: 105 and 118)

In this way, she warns against the use of gender analysis in education, which is not cross-referenced to issues of class and race. Her general thesis is that while middle-class girls (especially those attending single-sex urban schools) have made considerable progress in academic achievement and in entry to higher education, this is still not the case for many urban working-class girls.

Urban schools still face the challenge of encouraging working-class girls to realize their potential and to raise their career aspirations to the extent that their middle-class peers have demonstrated in recent decades. This challenge also applies to working-class boys. Urban schools are continuing to face challenging behaviours from boys characterized in the 1970s as The Lads (Willis 1977). The Lads represent a hardcore resistance by urban working-class boys to the educational mission of the school. This is not, as many commentators believe, a phenomenon of modern urban schooling. It has existed throughout the whole history of urban education (see Grace, 1978) and therefore it represents an enduring challenge. It can be seen as a contradiction of urban education because at the formal level the school holds out to these working-class boys, opportunities for personal and social fulfilment, improved life chances and career prospects and yet The Lads refuse these opportunities. Not only do they refuse these opportunities but also they engage in overt resistance designed to subvert school discipline, undermine the teachers and disrupt the learning environments of classrooms.

The contemporary urban school faces the challenge of 'how to reach, the hard to teach', and this 'hard' group is largely male. What has changed over time in urban schooling is the destinations of The Lads after school leaving age. In the past, many were destined for unskilled manual labour (and they knew this), whereas in a changed labour market their successors are destined for unemployment or recruitment into a growing urban crime and drug-dealing economy (and perhaps they know this). Whereas the contradictions of class in urban education have a long and well-documented history, the contradictions of gender have been in focus for a much shorter time.

Contradictions of race and ethnicity

Metropolitan cities are generally characterized by considerable ethnic and racial diversity, as various groups of people (for various reasons) are drawn to the opportunities, which the city appears to offer them and their families. Each of these 'new arrivals' to the city bring with them their particular cultural riches, religious and social practices, economic intelligence, and generally speaking, a strong desire (or need) to be 'successful' in their new environment. These characteristics have applied to successive waves of new arrivals in the city including: the Jews, the Irish, the Italians, the Chinese, the Afro-Caribbeans, Africans, Indians, Pakistani, Bangladeshi, Greek Cypriot, Turkish and, more recently, migrants from the new accession states to the EU from Eastern Europe and the Baltic region. These migrations have been further complicated by the arrival of refugee and asylum seekers as a result of conflicts taking place in many regions. The constant renewing of the city by the entry of these various ethnics groups has the potential to enrich and enhance urban culture, to stimulate its economy and to add new dimensions to its entrepreneurial activity, not to mention providing new recruits for the maintenance of its public services.

Racisms

The historically evident urban contradiction that works against the realization of many of these benefits is the existence, at the same time, of many forms of racism in the city. Thus the potential of the 'new arrivals' to enhance the city is constantly undermined by the presence of racisms which impede their contribution and which may provoke overt conflict. These contradictions of race are manifest in urban schooling in differing degrees according to complex circumstances. There has been a particular analytical focus in inner-city education contexts on the educational achievements of black students, defined in the US as Afro-Americans and in Britain as Afro-Caribbeans. Much of this debate focused on Intelligence Quotient (IQ) scores, and had significant racialist overtones. However, it is clear that if Black children were underachieving in inner-city schools it was more a function of their 'social circumstances' (which would include various forms of racism), than anything to do with innate limitations of their intelligence.

The Swann Committee subsequently made a strong statement on racism in its final report:

> [w]e believe that racism is an insidious evil which, for the sake of the future unity and stability of our society, must be countered. . . . Racism, in all its forms, needs to be tackled, in the interests of the community as a whole, since it damages not only the groups seen and treated as inferior but also the more powerful groups, in that it feeds them with a totally false sense of superiority. . . all members of a racist society suffer from feelings of fear and insecurity. . . . We believe that for schools to allow racist attitudes to persist unchecked constitutes a fundamental mis-education for their pupils. . . . We are convinced that the policies we put forward in this report will, if put into practice, mark a major change in the way in which ethnic minorities are perceived and perceive themselves in relation to the educational system. (36–7)

Stephen Lawrence and Anthony Walker

These disparities seem to be stubborn and enduring. The murders of Stephen Lawrence and Anthony Walker illustrate the evil and resistance of racism. Although the murder of the black teenager Stephen Lawrence in 1993 was far from being the first racially motivated murder, it was undoubtedly the first murder to have so many far-reaching and impacting implications. Without the unrelenting struggle of the Lawrences to fight for justice, there would have been no inquiry and ultimately no report (Macpherson, 1999). Although they targeted the police, the Macpherson (1999) recommendations were also explicit in their implications for the education system. For inner-city educators the challenges are enormous; the Citizenship Curriculum has been conceived to inform and educate children as to how to be active, informed, tolerant and responsible citizens. However, the murder of Anthony Walker in 2005, in circumstances chillingly similar to the death of Stephen Lawrence, raised the question as to whether citizenship is or can be a 'vehicle' that can have any impact on the racism that infiltrates our schools and colleges. In the 15 years since the Lawrence murder there has been escalating racial violence (race hate crimes have more than doubled in London to an average of 63 a day in the 12 months to April 2005 (*Guardian*, 19 June 2005) and in the borough of Huyton, Liverpool, where Anthony was murdered they have escalated to 53 reported racially motivated crimes in the period January to March 2005 (BBC News, 2 August 2005)).

In other words, institutional racism, understood to be how the interests and attitudes of a dominant race saturate the cultures and procedures of key institutions, is remarkably tenacious. Ultimately, government reports, research studies and educational programmes do not appear to be having much impact on the outcomes of institutional racism.

Contradictions of literacy

Metropolitan cities tend to act as magnets for the literacy resources of a society – its writers and poets, publishers and journalists, debaters, orators and public speakers, academics, lawyers and preachers. Manchester, the place where we began this chapter, has located itself as a Knowledge Capital, to a large extent built around its media city status. Cities concentrate the literate culture of the chattering classes, the writing classes and the public speaking classes into a powerful and richly varied network. It is characteristically the location of national and international media agencies. Yet this great literate resource co-exists with urban working-class and minority ethnic schools where literacy (understood as the ability to read and write and use language effectively) is still a significant challenge – despite recent literacy programmes.

The literacy challenges in inner-city schools have complex and deeply rooted causes. They include the enduring effects of a class strategy in English schooling that always limited the extent of literacy development for the working-class majority, while allowing 'sponsored literacy' for the scholarship elect. Literacy development had potentially serious implications for social control in a class society. The enduring consequences of this strategy have resulted in generations of working-class adults who have never achieved levels of competence and confidence (or enjoyment) in literate culture (in reading, writing and public speaking).

Many children and young people from these homes have attended inner-city schools where attempts to assist their progress in literacy have been impeded by class sizes, problems of teacher retention and inadequate programmes of teaching and learning. These challenges have been compounded by the fact that such schools receive successive waves of refugee and/or asylum-seeking children who place heavy demands upon the literacy resources available. This situation represents what may be called the contradiction of classic literacy (the differential command of reading, writing and public speaking). The importance of such classic literacy had long been recognized by elite public and private schools for the empowerment that it provides for their learners. Such schools have always understood that confidence and fluency in public speaking is an essential and not an optional part of literacy development. Inner-city working-class schools can learn from this historical tradition. New forms of communication, which demand new literacies, may well exacerbate this divide. For instance, a study of internet use among more than 1,500 youngsters, conducted by the London School of Economics, revealed that children from better-off backgrounds not only had greater access to the World Wide Web at home but were more likely to exploit its array of resources (Livingstone and Bober, 2005). Livingstone and Bober (2005) concluded that working-class children were losing out in the digital divide.

An assets-based approach to confronting the contradictions of inner-city education

In order for the contradictions of inner-city education, which arise out of the inequities present in the education system, to be confronted schools in the inner cities need to transform into the hubs of community development which exploit the assets present within the whole community. Cunningham and Mathie (2001) suggest a model of drawing upon community assets which is based on the principles of appreciating and mobilizing individual and community talents, skills and assets (rather than focusing on problems and needs). This is a community-driven development rather than development driven by external agencies. This 'Assets-Based Community Development' (ABCD) approach builds on:

- *Appreciative inquiry* which identifies and analyses the community's past successes. This strengthens people's confidence in their own capacities and inspires them to take action.
- The recognition of *social capital* and its importance as an asset. This is why ABCD focuses on the power of associations and informal linkages within the community, and the relationships built over time between community associations and external institutions.
- *Participatory approaches to development*, which are based on principles of empowerment and ownership of the development process.
- *Community economic development* models that place priority on collaborative efforts for economic development that makes best use of its own resource base.

- Efforts to strengthen *civil society*. These efforts have focused on how to engage people as citizens (rather than clients) in development, and how to make local governance more effective and responsive. (Cunningham and Mathie, 2001)

Self-mobilization for change

ABCD is a process of self-mobilization and organizing for change. This process has happened spontaneously in many communities. The challenge for an external agency, such as a Non-Governmental Organization (NGO), is to stimulate this process in other communities without having the opposite effect of creating dependency. There are a set of methods that can be used but they should be seen as guidelines not a blueprint for achieving community-driven development. ABCD draws upon collecting stories, organizing a core group, mapping the capacities and assets of individuals, associations and local institutions, building a community vision and plan, mobilizing and linking assets for economic development, and leveraging activities, investments and resources from outside the community.

The Developmental Asset framework

The Developmental Asset framework (Search Institute, 2005) is categorized into two groups of 20 assets. External assets are the positive experiences young people receive from the world around them. These 20 assets are about supporting and empowering young people, setting boundaries and expectations, and about positive and constructive use of young people's time. External assets identify important roles that families, schools, church groups, neighbourhoods and youth organizations can play in promoting healthy development. The 20 internal assets identify those characteristics and behaviours that reflect positive internal growth and development of young people. These assets are about positive values and identities, social competences, and commitment to learning. The internal Developmental Assets may help these young people make thoughtful and positive choices and, in turn, be better prepared for situations in life that challenge their inner strength and confidence.

The Search Institute has surveyed over 2 million young people across the United States and Canada since 1989, focusing on their experiences, attitudes, behaviours and the number of Developmental Assets at work for these young people. These studies reveal strong and consistent relationships between the number of assets present in young people's lives and the degree to which they develop in positive ways. The results show that the greater the numbers of Developmental Assets are experienced by young people, the more positive and successful are their development. The fewer the number of assets present, the greater the possibility youth will engage in risky behaviours such as drug use, unsafe sex and violence (Search Institute, 2005). The Search Institute argues that the reality is that the average young person surveyed in the US experiences only 18 of the 40 assets. Overall, 62 per cent of young people surveyed have fewer than 20 of the 40 assets.

In short, the majority of young people in the US, from all walks of life, are lacking in sufficient Developmental Assets needed for healthy development. These statistics, as well as the role assets play in predicting both positive and negative outcomes for youth, underscore the importance of the Developmental Asset framework and its application (Search Institute, 2005).

Conclusion

At one level, the city has the potential of providing a wide array of resources to its inhabitants. For example, high levels of diversity commensurate with the metropolitan areas brings a richness of experience that enables a dynamic synthesis of the creative, scientific and cultural into new forms of working, enterprise development and employment opportunities. Cities are increasingly marketing themselves as knowledge and informational cities that can harness the creative forces of various sectors into a hub of expertise and excellence with the potential for growth and global economic competitiveness. Cities are the hub of economic activity for whole city regions.

However, living cheek by jowl with this rich panoply of social, cultural, economic, employment and infrastructural possibilities, cities contain many profound pockets of economic disadvantage and poverty. These levels of disadvantage and poverty manifest themselves in many different ways. For example, whole communities that may once have had clear links to the historical manufacturing and production identity of the city now find they lack appropriate skills for new city economies. Many of those that have been able to up-skill and change have moved on resulting in the net migration out of areas of decline. The many communities that remain are beset with endemic and polarized levels of deprivation clearly indicated by high levels of unemployment, crime and disorder, problems with drug misuse and health concerns. Local housing and shopping precincts may have become run down and many families struggle to maintain structure, expectations, aspiration and esteem within such contexts. Furthermore, race, class and gender inequalities cut across many of these issues and continue to reinforce barriers to achievement.

Perhaps more insidiously, these structural inequalities help to constrain the opportunity for individuals to develop the types of emotional, intellectual, cultural and social capital needed to bridge the gap into the many opportunities provided by the city. Indeed instead of creating opportunities for individual development that are based on the city's rich diversity there are many examples of differences being exploited with enhanced community fragmentation and prejudice. As a result of some of these issues, young people and their families and communities become socially excluded and disengaged from many of the opportunities that the city can offer. Most significantly for educators, many young people then underachieve in schooling and struggle to make an effective transition to adulthood and work.

Formal and informal educational institutions

Formal and informal educational institutions in the city reflect this complex and dynamic milieu. They therefore face increasing challenges and have to meet a diverse set of needs if they are to achieve the goals of educational development and improvement of all young people and the communities which they serve. Indeed much government policy has concerned itself with attempting to enable educational institutions to become the lead player, working alongside other public service provision, in ameliorating the position of young people and their communities. Hence a number of interrelated and competing push/pull factors appear to be informing the strategic configuration and the emerging policy and practice of educational provision in many cities. At least three imperatives face educational institutions in the city in trying to develop educational programmes for citizens living in the twenty-first century:

- There is the imperative of *achievement for all*. This is certainly about the core educational concern of attainment within a formal curriculum. However, in many cities it is also about a wider notion of achievement which includes the development of personal, social and employment-related skills as well as an understanding of citizenship issues. It is often also about an inclusive view of achievement in which the effectiveness of the education system is judged not just by the achievements of the few, or even of the many, but of all learners.
- There is the imperative of *child and family well-being*. Education both depends on and contributes to the well-being of learners and their families. Physical and mental health, family function and dysfunction are concerns which education services cannot afford to ignore.
- There is the imperative of *community regeneration*. This is the extent to which the urban economy thrives, what employment opportunities are available and how well-equipped people are to take advantage of them. It is also concerned with the quality and type of housing, the availability of transport to extend people's opportunities, the safety and cohesion of communities and, ultimately, about the quality of life in communities and neighbourhoods.

Cutting across imperatives

Cutting across each of these imperatives are issues to do with the nature of the communities which make up the city. These often concern race, class, culture and gender. They are also to do with politics, governance and voice – that is, with the relationship between policy and practice on the one hand and the needs and wishes of community members on the other.

Different cities respond to these imperatives in different ways. For some, the most pressing imperative is to deliver elementary education for all and this may mean capitalizing on informal educational networks. For others, the key issue is schools and, specifically, the drop-out, disengagement and disaffection of many young people which makes the system unable to deliver achievement for all. For others again, the role of education in economic development and regeneration is key and tertiary education is at least as important as schooling.

However, what is not clear in the context of the challenges and imperatives identified above is what inner-city education is or might be, and how it differs from other forms of education to be found outside the urban areas. We have deliberately chosen not to try to answer this question, as we have indicated earlier. Other, perhaps more relevant questions than trying to define inner-city education, focus on how different socio-cultural and historical perspectives give rise to different responses to the urban educational challenges in different spaces and places. Lines of cleavage in different cities have responded to these differing cultural and historical perspectives and lineages in different ways, some around issues of race and racial difference, others around issues of ethnicity and ethnic diversity. At least two forms of response to these questions may be identified. One clusters around deficit or pathological models of education, predicated on the assumption that urban dwellers face educational deficits that need to be 'fixed' and that the solution lies in finding the right fix for the right problem. The other clusters around an assets model of education, which argues that the answer to the urban challenge lies in harnessing the assets of the particular community in a particular place at a particular time. Different cities, in different cultural places, with different historical influences and different local, state/regional or national/federal policy imperatives have responded to these challenges and imperatives in different ways.

Learning institutions and community

The main ingredients and/or requirements for changing and improving lives involve putting the child at the centre of the transformational process. Learning institutions must create a greater sense of community. They must listen to the child's voice and to the community to avoid unnecessary duplication. Learning institutions need to be (re)conceptualized as community hubs, the co-location for services to enhance access, provide parenting support, working with a transformed and transformational curriculum. The key to success is early intervention, starting with the child, as early as birth. Educational reform will require three strategies: a paradigm of redistribution – wealth must be redistributed to provide greater equity; a paradigm of recognition – individuals must be seen as valuable people with a clear sense of their own chosen identities; and a paradigm of representation – all classes of people in the cultural mix of the community must have a voice. All members of urban communities must be accepted and given the opportunity to learn and prosper in the community and in society. Education must be the instrument to achieve this transformation.

Key Points

- Education in the inner cities in the UK exhibit the widest disparities between the highest and lowest achievers academically

⇨

- Though differences exist in other areas it is the concentration and degree of difference that is unique to the inner city
- Inner cities also exhibit inequalities in terms of access to education
- The underachievement by significant numbers of inner-city children is enduring and impacts on large numbers of families
- There is a strong correlation between economic disadvantage and educational attainment
- There have been a number of government initiatives to address the issue of underachievement of the poorest sections of society – they have met with limited success
- The link between poverty and educational attainment impacts on all children, whether they are white working-class or from ethnic minority backgrounds
- The inner city is characterized by a number of contradictions centred around power and the control of resources – education is a key element in this conflict
- The key contradictions are:
  - Class
  - Gender
  - Race and ethnicity
  - Literacy
- An alternative response to the issues encountered in inner cities is to develop an Assets-Based Community Development (ABCD) programme. This approach is driven by the community rather than top-down government action
- The ABCD approach is based on five key elements:
  - Appreciative inquiry – identifies past achievements in the community
  - Social capital – recognition of the strengths in the community
  - Participatory approaches to development – empowerment in the community
  - Community economic development – models collaboration
  - Civil society – encourages social and political engagement
- Cities have a vast array of resources that can challenge the structural inequalities in society, key to this is the formal and informal education institutions
- Overcoming disadvantage must be centred around:
  - Achievement for all
  - Child and family well-being
  - Community regeneration.

Further Reading

Castells, M. (1997) *The Urban Question*, London: Edward Arnold.

David Gillborn (1995) *Racism and Antiracism in Real Schools*, Maidenhead: Open University Press.

Hirsch, D. (2007) *Experiences of Poverty and Educational Disadvantage*, Joseph Rowntree Foundation, www.jrf.org.uk, September 2007.

Stuart Weir (ed.) (2006) *Unequal Britain*, London: Politicos.

Note

1. We wish to express our gratitude to Gerald Grace for the material which forms the basis of this section of the chapter.

References

Blanden, J. and Machin, S. (2007) *Recent Changes in Intergenerational Mobility in the UK: A Summary of Findings*, London: Sutton Trust.

Carvel, J. (2007) *Class Divide Hits Learning Age by Three*, http://education.guardian.co.uk/schools/story/0,,2100041,00.html [accessed 11 June 2007].

Castells, M. (1997) *The Urban Question*, London: Edward Arnold.

Cunningham, G. and Mathie, A. (2001) 'Asset-Based Community Development: An Overview', paper prepared for the ABCD Workshop, organized by Synergos on 21 February, 2002 in Bangkok, Thailand, www.synergos.org/global-philanthropy/02/abcdoverview.htm [accessed 4 Jan. 2009].

Department of Children, Schools and Families (DCSF) (2008) *Raising the Bar, Closing the Gap: A Vision and Operational Strategy for the Greater Manchester Challenge*, London: DCSF.

Department for Education and Skills (DfES) (2003) *The London Challenge: Transforming London Secondary Schools*, London: DfES.

Galbraith, J. (1992) *The Culture of Contentment*, London: Sinclair-Stevenson.

Grace, G. (1978) *Teachers, Ideology and Control: Study in Urban Education*, London: Routledge and Kegan Paul.

Grace, G. (1994) 'Urban education and the culture of contentment', in N. Stromquist (ed.), *Education in Urban Areas: Cross-National Dimensions*, Westpoint, CT: Praeger.

Grace, G. (2006) 'Urban education: confronting the contradictions', paper presented to the Facing the Urban Challenge: Educating in the Cities for the 21st Century International Invitation Seminar, Manchester, University of Manchester and Manchester Metropolitan University, Centre for Urban Education, December 2006.

Hirsch, D. (2007) *Experiences of Poverty and Educational Disadvantage*, Joseph Rowntree Foundation, www.jrf.org.uk, September 2007.

Institute of Education (2007) 'Disadvantaged children up to a year behind by the age of three', Centre for Longitudinal Studies, London, University of London Institute of Education, www.cls.ioe.ac.uk/news.asp?section=000100010003&item=409 [accessed 11 June 2007].

Livingstone, S. and Bober, M. (2005) *UK Children Go Online: Final Report to the Economic and Social Research Council*, London: LSE.

Macpherson, W. (1999) *The Stephen Lawrence Inquiry* (The Macpherson Report), Cmnd. 4262-I, London: The Stationery Office.

Merson, M. W. and Campbell, R. J. (1974) 'Community education: instruction for inequality', *Journal of Education for Teaching*, no. 93.

Raffo, C. (2006) 'Education, poverty and the urban context: mapping the terrain and making the links to educational policy', paper presented to the Facing the Urban Challenge: Educating in the Cities for the 21st Century International Invitation Seminar, Manchester, University of Manchester and Manchester Metropolitan University, Centre for Urban Education, December 2006.

Reay, D. (2003) 'Reproduction, reproduction, reproduction: Troubling dominant discourses on education and social class in the UK', in J. Freeman-Moir and A. Scott (eds), *Yester-day's Dreams: International and Critical Perspectives on Education and Social Class*, New Zealand: University of Canterbury Press, pp. 104–22.

Search Institute (2005) *Developmental Asset Framework*, Minneapolis: Search Institute.

Social Exclusion Unit (SEU) (1998) *Bringing Britain Together: A National Strategy for Neighbourhood Renewal*, Cm 4045, London: The Stationery Office.

Swann Report (1985) *Education for All*, London: HMSO.

Walters, M. (2007) 'Engaging urban learners', paper presented to the Engaging Urban learners Conference, Manchester, Manchester Metropolitan University, Centre for Urban Education, June 2007.

Whitty, G. (2002) *Making Sense of Education Policy*, London: Paul Chapman Publishing.

Part Three
Global Issues

Learning from Europe: Social pedagogy and looked-after children

Derek Kassem

9

Introduction

Every Child Matters (ECM) is at the forefront of the government's agenda and to a certain extent, with some variation, the agenda of the opposition parties as well. A key element of the ECM agenda is meeting the needs of those children who are described as being looked after. These are children for whom the state is the surrogate parent. They are in the care of local authorities, in many ways because the government has highlighted the position and plight of looked-after children. They act as a litmus test for the efficacy of the ECM agenda, for failing to address the most highlighted group's needs would indicate that there is something not quite right with the way that ECM is actually being implemented. The reality for many of these children is that the state in the UK is a poor parent, especially if levels of educational achievement and life chances are employed as an indicator of welfare. This chapter will outline the difficulties that face looked-after children, before rehearsing a discussion of the approach that is adopted by a number of countries within Europe that achieve far greater life chances for similar such children. In the process of examining the approach taken in Europe, the chapter will first analyse then compare the level of training and qualifications that professionals working with looked-after children have in both the UK and Europe. Coupled with this, the chapter will further discuss the practice of a more holistic, social pedagogy adopted within Europe.

Pedagogy is a term not often used by practitioners within education, and social pedagogy is a concept that is not used at all by practitioners in the UK. However, it is an approach that considers the needs of the whole child and which does not distinguish between their social and educational needs, as tends to be the common practice in the UK. It will be asserted that this approach to the needs of looked-after children has something to teach practitioners in the UK, be they social workers, teachers or anyone in fact who works with looked-after children. The underlying issue is that the needs of looked-after children can be significantly enhanced by this approach to their care. It might also be the case that a similar approach to the needs of children who face any number of difficulties would result in their needs being met more effectively than current practice actually allows.

Useful Websites

Every Child Matters ECM website on looked-after children	www.everychildmatters.gov.uk/ socialcare/childrenincare/research/
Who cares trust Leading charity working with looked-after children	www.thewhocarestrust.org.uk/
Voice Voice is one of the UK's leading voluntary organizations working and campaigning for children and young people in public care	www.voiceyp.org/ngen_public/ default.asp
Network of children's rights officers and advocates	www.croa.org.uk/

Some terms and definitions – what 'looked after' means

Looked-after children is the term used to describe those children who are cared for by the state, in the UK this means the Local Authority (LA), in one form or another. This may mean care in a local authority children's home, foster care or otherwise in secure accommodation. However, this list does little justice to the varied forms that placements actually take, for instance foster care may mean a child is looked after by a family unit in which the foster child is the only child in care. Equally, foster care may mean the child is one of many 'foster children' looked after in a community run on a private basis, funded by the LA.

Reasons for entering the care system

The reasons for a child entering care are as varied as the forms of care themselves. One important point, is that less than 10 per cent of children in state care are there because of their own behaviour (SEU, 2003) or because they will not attend school. It is worth noting that since the passing of the Children Act (1989), education departments have lost their right to start care proceedings. Most children thus end up in care because they are in need of care and protection for one reason or another: family breakdown; abuse, both sexual and physical; neglect and emotional abuse; death of parents or for social reasons within the family that result in the child entering the care system on a voluntary basis. What is known is that children are more likely to enter the care system if they come from one-parent families, a poor household, live in overcrowded accommodation or are from a mixed heritage background (Statham et al., 2002). However, what must be remembered is that, no matter what the background or stated reason, a child entering care suffers a double disadvantage. First, the actual process of going into care is frequently a harrowing experience for the child because of family breakdown or abuse. Second, being in care is itself a disadvantage as indicated below. It is the child's own personal 'double whammy', to borrow a well-used election slogan.

Indicators of educational achievement

The numbers of looked-after children are comparatively small compared with the child population as a whole. In 2006, there were 44,200 children who had been in continuous care of a local authority for the previous 12 months. Of these, 34,000 were children of school age. A proportion of 28 per cent of the children attending school had Special Education Needs (SEN) statements and 1 per cent had received a permanent exclusion (DfES, 2007). The level of achievement by looked-after children does not compare well with the general population, for instance, only 63 per cent of looked-after children obtained at least one GCSE or GNVQ compared with 98 per cent of school children overall (DfES, 2007). In terms of government targets for all children, only 12 per cent obtained at least five GCSE (or equivalent) at grades A*–C compared with 59 per cent of the general population (DfES, 2007). A total of 34 per cent did not sit exams and thus left school with no qualifications. The lack of any form of qualifications on leaving school may offer a partial explanation for the comparatively high levels of unemployment of school leavers in care compared with those leaving school within the general population. For example, looked-after children had an unemployment rate of 20 per cent compared to a figure of just 5 per cent for all children (DfES, 2007).

Stop, Read and Reflect

An experience of the care system and school

Alex Skyes was in care and has worked in menial jobs since leaving school. He said,

> For my first two years in secondary school I was the only one who was in care. Everyone knew because the children's home was up the road. The whole thing felt alien to me.
>
> By year 10 I did not bother to go to school much. In year 11 I managed to get a job working in a hotel through work experience so I spent most of my time there. (*Times Educational Supplement,* 13 January 2006)

Alex Skyes has since been diagnosed as dyslexic, his experiences of the care system and the consequences are typical for many children in care.

Question

1. To what extent would a holistic approach to the education and needs of looked-after children address the problems faced by Alex?

Problems encountered

The difficulties that looked-after children face, in terms of their education, effectively puts them at the bottom of society's education achievement stakes. For example, only one in a hundred looked-after children enter university, compared with 43 per cent of all children (Jackson et al., 2005), and only 8 per cent of looked-after children obtained five GCSEs A*–C grade, compared to over half of the whole population in 2005 (ibid.).

One recent study (Fletcher-Campbell and Archer, 2003) found that the greater the number of placements, that is, in terms of where a child lives, increases the level of instability in the child's life and also the number of schools they attend. Children who change schools frequently not only repeat a lot of their learning, but are also less likely to be entered for formal academic assessments. Quite simply, the school may not have the information about the child to make an informed judgement about which exam a child may possibly be entered for, so quite frequently they are not entered for any at all. In these days of league tables, with increased auditing and accountability, the logic from the school's point of view is hard to fault, for exams represent high stakes for schools in terms of funding and status. It can be noted that children who are labelled as educational failures by the system, which looked-after children are often perceived to be, are rarely considered assets to their school.

It is possible to argue that for a child who is looked after, the ability to just stay in school represents a considerable achievement, as such children are ten times more likely to be excluded from school than the school population as a whole. In fact, one recent study indicated 32 per cent of children in care were reported as being excluded from school (Armstrong et al., 2005).

Life chances

The overall poor levels of academic achievement by children in care do not diminish once they leave care. Research into the outcomes for children who have left the care system has constantly produced findings that show that they remain educationally disadvantaged and that this, in turn, often leads to disadvantage in other areas of their lives (Hayden et al., 1999). The life chances of those who have been in care present a frequently gloomy reality; for example, between 25 per cent and a third of so-called rough sleepers were identified as being in care (SEU, 2003). This figure is similar to the one identified by *The Big Issue*, who found around 18 per cent of their vendors had been in care at some point in their lives (Big Issue, 2001). Similarly, around a quarter of adults in prison have spent some of their childhood in care (SEU, 2002) and children in care are two-and-half times more likely to become teenage parents (SEU, 1999). Furthermore, in one study by the Home Office into vulnerable people (Cusick et al., 2003), it was found that 42 per cent of sex workers interviewed had spent some period of their childhood in care. The same study also found similar rates for drug users. This is not to say, of course, that all children who have been through the care system have unsuccessful lives, quite the contrary, but a great many do have problems in later life due in part to poor education.

Activity

1. What factors do you think cause looked-after children to have such poor life chances?
2. What would you advocate to change this situation?

Residential care

In the UK, only a minority of looked-after children are placed in residential care, a Children's Home or similar institution. The number of children who live in residential care in the UK is substantially lower than in countries such as Denmark, France, Germany and the Netherlands (Petrie et al., 2006). Although one of the difficulties in using comparative data is that there is a variation in definitions of care and in how data is collected, as Petrie (2003) states, the difference in the figures is striking. This is perhaps due to the way in which policy has been followed by successive UK governments: of closing down Children's Homes and moving to foster care. Within the UK context, the reasons for the use of foster care are varied but include the high cost of running residential institutions and quality of care that is available. In addition, more recently it has come to light that there were a number of sex abuse scandals in residential institutions in the 1970s and 1980s. Foster care was thus seen as an attempt to meet the needs of looked-after children by replicating the family unit, in other words, giving the children the experiences that they were clearly missing.

Residential care in the European context

Residential care of children in the UK has been plagued by a number of different concerns and issues for some considerable time (see previous page) and seems somewhat resistant to change (Petrie and Simon, 2006). In part, this may be a product of the status that residential care has in the UK compared with our near European neighbours. In the UK, residential care is often the choice of last resort, when all else fails or otherwise as a means of emergency. However, this is not the case for Germany or Denmark. As British social policy has focused on foster care rather than residential care as a solution to the needs of looked-after children, those living in residential care are often seen as more 'difficult' and challenging (ibid.). However, foster care is often difficult to obtain, for there is always a shortage and sometimes it is simply inappropriate. The quality of what is provided by foster carers varies considerably and is seemingly always to the detriment of children.

In Germany, the relationship a child has with residential care is substantially different to that in the UK. In part, this reflects the different perspectives towards care, an approach through the use of pedagogy and, in particular, social pedagogy that exists within the practice of our European neighbours. In the UK, one is either in foster care or in a Children's Home, there is no link between the two settings. However, in Germany the child may continue to use residential services, in some cases well into their twenties (Petrie and Simon, 2006) and continue to receive support from those practitioners working in residential care. In many ways this process replicates the experience of the family in the wider population, for example, the process of leaving home is frequently a long and protracted affair with children often returning home for different lengths of time, be it for short visits or slightly longer stays. What is also notable in terms of adults working with looked-after children is the nomenclature used to describe them: in the UK it is often 'practitioner' and in countries such as Germany it is 'pedagogue'. The very terms indicate a marked difference in status.

Staff qualifications

In contrast with Europe in which greater emphasis is placed on residential care, UK policy tends to focus predominantly on foster care, which impacts on the level of training that is available to, and expected of, those working in residential care. In Germany, the level of qualification needed to work as a 'pedagogue' obtains to a university level education (Petrie and Simon, 2006), lasting approximately four and a half years. This provides the adult with a diploma in social pedagogy. There are lower level qualifications but they neither have the same status nor title. The least qualified is that of Erzieher (up-bringer), however, this still takes three years to achieve.

Denmark is similar to Germany in that one must be qualified to work as a pedagogue; indeed, the majority of staff working in residential care are also similarly qualified. The qualification takes three and a half years to achieve and the course includes working in a wide range of settings with different children (Petrie et al., 2006). Significantly, students are trained to work with children with a range of problems, including disabilities, alcohol and substance abuse. In terms of the UK, these issues are also of concern. For instance, 5 per cent of looked-after children have been identified as a substance misuse problem (DfES, 2007). However, when one turns to assess the level of training and qualifications required to work in residential care in the UK, the picture is radically different.

UK staff training and qualifications

The approach taken in the UK is that of 'on-the-job' training through the National Vocational Qualification (NVQ) award. Yet the reality is that many residential care practitioners do not have any qualifications or training other than what is often coyly referred to as 'life training'. Moreover, the approach taken by the NVQ is a competency-based approach judged against a set of benchmarks or national standards. However, this training does not seem to have any beneficial outcomes for the children in residential care (Whittaker et al., 1998 cited in Petrie and Simon, 2006). Direct comparison draws the stark reality in the differences that exist between the UK and countries such as Germany and Denmark:

- English workers: 26 per cent held the NVQ level 3
- Danish workers: 76 per cent held a pedagogy qualification (degree level, obtained over three years)
- German workers: 57 per cent of workers held the Erzieher qualifications (obtained over three years post-compulsory schooling), 26 per cent had obtained a pedagogy qualification, obtained over three years at degree level in a Fachochschule (higher education institution) and 6 per cent held a university diploma degree in social pedagogy at around the level of a Masters degree. (Petrie and Simon, 2006: 122)

Pertie and Simon (2006) also point out that for the most part English practitioners work with children who are more disadvantaged than their German and Danish counterparts and yet have fewer qualifications and less training experience.

Social pedagogy

The education, rather than training, that German and Danish pedagogues receive is rooted in the concept of social pedagogy, for which there is no single or unitary definition (Paget et al., 2007). The word pedagogy itself is rarely used outside the academic world in the UK, however, in Continental Europe it is:

often used to relate to the education of the whole person: body, mind, feelings spirit, creativity and, crucially, the relationship of the individual to others. (Petrie, 2003: 63)

The origins of social pedagogy

The origins of social pedagogy, Petrie (2003) suggests, are to be found in the work of Mager, a nineteenth-century German pedagogue, who defined social pedagogy in much broader terms than it is usually defined in the UK. The English-speaking world thinks of pedagogy in terms of what might be termed the science of teaching. This clearly locates pedagogy in the classroom and is linked to the curriculum. For those located within Continental Europe, however, the notion of social pedagogy is far removed from this limited definition; it relates to the whole child and places that child in the context of the wider society. Thus theory, policy and practice can be regarded as the integrated parts of a process of training the social pedagogue. Accordingly, pedagogy for the social pedagogue can be described as:

> being concerned with the formation of the personality, acquisition of social competences, moral guidance, the securing of independence and a capacity for self-regulation and the ability to join in the social, political and cultural life of the adult community. Social pedagogues help promote personal and social development. Their skills and commitment enable them to work with all types of people and not only those identified as problem groups. (Jones, 2000 cited in Paget et al., 2007: 8)

Differences

This view of social pedagogy goes way beyond any of the approaches taken within the UK to the education of practitioners who work in residential care. It would also explain the different role that residential care has in Germany and Denmark, where clearly, there is strong emphasis on the child and a desire to understand the situation of the child. This is a far cry from the competency-based approach that is adopted in the UK. In many ways the very word 'training' indicates the status of what is provided in terms of education for residential care workers. As mentioned above, no formal qualifications are required for an individual to obtain employment in a Children's Home. The wholesale lack of any theoretical and/or policy perspective for these workers is not so dissimilar to what has happened within teacher education, often now referred to as a form of training based on competencies and without any real links to theory (Ball, 2008).

Defining social pedagogy

As already indicated, there is no single, universal definition of social pedagogy. The Social Education Trust (2001 cited in Paget et al., 2007) has identified some key characteristics of workers operating within social pedagogy practice, in that they:

> • often share the life-space of the children or young people they work with, whether in the child's environment, in the family home or community, or in a substitute environment such as a residential school, children's home or foster home;

- work generally in teams and as individual workers and therefore have to be capable of functioning effectively as team members;
- not only help children and young people develop as individuals but also as social beings who will be capable of contributing positively and fulfilling responsible roles as adults in the wider community;
- work towards the creation of a community which is worthy of children and young people as they develop towards maturity;
- often work outside, but link with, both the families and schools of the children with whom they work, though others are school based;
- may work with children and young people of any age and with any type of 'presenting problem', including physical and learning disabilities, social, emotional and mental health problems and offending;
- are expected to be imaginative and creative in finding ways of helping children to develop and overcome problems;
- view a child's situation holistically, including all aspects of their lives in assessing their situations, planning to meet their needs and working with them;
- focus primarily on the normal development of children with whom they work and see problems which children have within the wider context of the areas in which they normally function;
- are seen in some countries as having their own professional identity, distinct from social work, teaching, youth work, psychology, nursing or other established professions. (10)

Petrie et al. (2005 cited in Paget et al., 2007) identify some key characteristics of social pedagogues, the most important of which is the focus on the child as a whole person, along with the worker seeing themselves in a relationship with the child. The most important element of any social pedagogy is a firm commitment to the rights of the child that go well beyond the merely legalistic and procedural, in order to recognize their rights and needs. All this, of course, is beyond the training that is currently undertaken by a minority of residential care workers within the UK.

The educational experience

No matter what their circumstances, it is an indubitable fact that looked-after children face many difficulties. Indeed, the very fact they are in care is a major disadvantage, never mind the experiences they went through in the process of going into care. Thus, it should be stated that regardless of location there is no perfect system, either in the UK or elsewhere. The Germans and the Danes, for example, all have problems and not all the children who are looked after by the state in those specified countries actually succeed. Undoubtedly, education is a key issue for all looked-after children, yet as evidence in the UK shows, for the most part they still fail. In Continental Europe, the social pedagogue has a key role to play in the education of the child, in terms of exhibiting commitment and support to the whole child. In a study by Petrie and Simon (2006), there is evidence to suggest that while 60 per cent of German youngsters and 74 per cent of Danes had discussed their school attendance with a member of staff, less than 45 per cent of English children had benefited from a similar conversation. They also found that English children of school age were more likely to be outside the education system compared to their German and Danish counterparts.

In terms of education, the most important issue identified by Petrie and Simon (2006) is that although in all countries children under review had a large number of issues to face and could present challenging behaviour in an educational setting, over 46 per cent of English heads perceived the problems facing the child as being located within the child (i.e. their 'lack'), compared to only 20 per cent of German and 25 per cent of Danish heads. This is rather like blaming the victim and not recognizing the structural and institutional problems faced by children. This response provides compelling evidence of the level and extent of discrimination faced by looked-after children (Kassem, 2006), and more importantly indicates the inherent lack of understanding on the part of so-called, qualified professionals.

Social care

The same study (Petrie and Simon, 2006) found that the attitudes of children towards the members of staff that cared for them were different between all three countries but most stark between the UK and the others. On key issues such as being listened to, only 39 per cent of UK youngsters felt listened-to compared with 56 per cent of Germans and 97 per cent of Danish children. Moreover, only 40 per cent of UK youngsters felt that staff were supportive of their needs compared to 94 per cent and 97 per cent, in German and Danish contexts, respectively. Although the UK did not always underperform compared with its neighbours, overall there was a major difference in type, structure and quality of education. The difference lies not just in the numbers that are qualified, but also the duration and level to which they have been educated. As mentioned above, one of the most important differences is the status of residential care workers in this country; it remains persistently low and for the most part badly rewarded.

Foster care and education

As the majority of children in care in this country fail and most are placed in foster care, the level of education achieved by foster carers must be called into question. Indeed, one of the major factors in the poor level of educational performance of looked-after children in foster care is the complete lack of education and training experience of foster carers. As with children in residential care, the education of children in foster care is often not a major concern for carers or the social workers (Kassem, 2006). The reality is that looked-after children's services are 'done on the cheap'. The whole system is thus a 'Cinderella service'. It should be recognized that the reasons for moving to a model of foster care were based on both the cost and the scandal of abuse within the residential care system. Both of these elements continue to reflect the lack of social, political and economic investment in the system that exists to this day.

Activity

The UK policy of using foster care as the primary method of caring for looked-after children has a number of implications for their care and education.

1. Can you identify the issues that arise out of this policy for looked-after children in the following areas:
   - Education
   - Social care
   - Life chances
   - Leaving care.

Conclusion

The approach taken in Europe to the needs of looked-after children has a great deal to teach the UK. The way in which the needs of the child are linked together by a holistic approach is the basis of addressing some of inequalities that they face. By far, the most significant factor that might be considered is the required level and quality of education received by care workers. Care workers in the UK, whether in residential homes or otherwise foster placements, often receive the bare minimum, if any, training. This has a major impact on their ability to identify and address the needs of young people with whom they are working and caring for. While there have been changes recently to the system, the young person is often still left to fend for themselves at a very early age with all the attendant problems this engenders. The ongoing relationship that the social pedagogue develops with a child, allowing the child to return to the care setting as and when needed until their early twenties, is a support mechanism sadly absent in the UK. The changes that are truly required to address the needs of looked-after children in the UK are fundamental and will take an order of political and social will well beyond the current level of policy rhetoric of ECM.

All social and caring services within the UK are dominated by government targets that specifically apply to each role. The targets for looked-after children, for example, are linked both to their social care and educational targets, for social workers and teachers respectively. The consequence of this, of course, is that different professionals, with different roles, are frequently working in different directions (Kassem, 2006). In terms of ECM, which is supposed to promote inter-agency or multi-agency working between professionals, the tendency towards identified targets creates a somewhat insurmountable barrier. The rhetoric of policy is highly laudable but on an operational level it seems not to come together. For example, teachers are more concerned with meeting targets for SATs tests and performing well in league tables, while the social worker is more concerned with targets for the placement of the child. In the process, children are failing to receive the holistic and integrated support they need and thus continue to suffer and fail, being let down by the system. Currently only 1 per cent of children who are looked after make entry to university. This compares with the government's target of 50 per cent for the population at large, and goes some way to demonstrating the sheer scale of the problem. If a major change is not made in the care system soon, more generations of children in care are likely to be condemned to educational failure.

Key Points

- The ECM agenda is a major government initiative aimed at addressing the needs of children
- A key group within the ECM agenda is looked-after children. The ability of ECM to overcome the problems faced by this group of children could be considered a litmus test for the whole initiative
- The educational experience of looked-after children is characterized by failure
- The subsequent lives of looked-after children is often one of social exclusion
- Residential care of looked-after children is in decline within the UK due to issues such as cost and pervious scandals. In Europe, residential care is the main mechanism for caring for children who are in the care of the state
- Compared with the rest of Europe, the UK has one of the worst records in meeting the needs of looked-after children
- The training and education of staff who work with looked-after children in Europe is substantially greater than in the UK. In fact an individual does not need any qualifications other than life skills to work in a children's home in the UK
- The approach taken to the needs of looked-after children in Europe is social pedagogy
- Social pedagogy is a holistic, ongoing supportive approach to the needs of looked-after children
- Social pedagogues live and work with looked-after children and maintain contact after the child has left residential care
- The approach is aimed at meeting the developmental needs of children
- The rhetoric of ECM suggests a holistic approach to the needs of the child but on an operational level it is dominated by the targets set by government for the various professions that work with looked-after children
- ECM is failing to meet the needs of looked-after children and the situation of most looked-after children is not improving.

Further Reading

Chase, E., Simon, A. and Jackson, S. (eds) (2006) *In Care and after a Positive Perspective*, London: Routledge.

Jeune Guishard-Pine, Suzanne McCall and Lloyd Hamilton (2007) *Understanding Looked After Children*, London: Jessica Kingsley Publishers.

Paolo Hewitt (2002) *The Looked After Kid – My Life in a Children's Home*, London: Mainstream Publishing.

Petrie, P., Boddy, J., Camerson, C., Wigfall, V. and Simon, A. (2006) *Working with Children in Care*, Maidenhead: Open University Press.

References

Armstrong, D., Hine, J., Armaos, R., Jones, R., Klessinger, N. and France, A. (2005) *Children, Risk and Crime: The On Track Youth Lifestyles Surveys*, London: Home Office.

Ball, S. (2008) *The Education Debate*, Bristol: Policy Press.

Big Issue (2001) *10th Birthday Survey* September edition, London: Big Issue.

Cusick, L., Martin, A. and May, T. (2003) *Vulnerability and Involvement in Drug Use and Sex Work*, London: Home Office.

Department for Education and Skills (DfES) (2007) *Outcome Indicators for Looked After Children: Twelve Months to 30th September 2006*, London: DfES.

Fletcher-Campbell, F. and Archer, T. (2003) *Achievement at Key Stage 4 of Young Children in Public Care*, London: DfES.

Hayden, C., Goddard, J., Gorrin, S. and Van Der Spek, N. (1999) *State Child Care Looking After Children?* London: Jessica Kingsley Publishers.

Jackson, S., Ajayi, S. and Quigley, M. (2005) *Going to University from Care*, London: University of London Institute of Education.

Kassem, D. (2006) 'Education of looked-after children: who cares?' in D. Kassem, E. Mufti and J. Robinson (eds), *Education Studies Issues and Critical Perspectives*, Maidenhead: Open University Press.

Paget, B., Eagle, G. and Citarella, V. (2007) *Social Pedagogy and the Young People's Workforce: A Report for the Department for Children, Schools and Families*, Liverpool: CPEA.

Petrie, P. (2003) 'Social pedagogy: an historical account of care and education as social control', in J. Brannen and P. Moss (eds), *Rethinking Children's Care*, Maidenhead: Open University Press.

Petrie, P. and Simon, A. (2006) 'Residential care: lessons from Europe', in E. Chase, A. Simon and S. Jackson (eds), *In Care and after: A Positive Perspective*, London: Routledge.

Petrie, P., Boddy, J., Cameron, C., Heptinstall, E., McQuail, S., Simon, A. and Wigfall, V. (2005) *Pedagogy – A Holistic, Personal Approach to Work with Children and Young People across Services*, Briefing Paper, June 2005, Thomas Coram Research Unit www.k1.ioe.ac.uk/tcru/PedBriefingPaper.pdf [accessed 31 July 2008].

Petrie, P., Boddy, J., Cameron, C., Wigfall, V. and Simon, A. (2006) *Working with Children in Care: European Perspectives*, Maidenhead: Open University Press

Social Education Trust (2001) *Social Pedagogy and Social Education* [Formerly known as the Radisson Report] Children UK, March 2001 www.childrenuk.co.uk/chmar2001/index.htm [accessed 31 July 2008].

Social Exclusion Unit (SEU) (1999) *Teenage Pregnancy*, London: SEU.

Social Exclusion Unit (SEU) (2002) *Reducing Re-offending by Ex-prisoners*, London: SEU.

Social Exclusion Unit (SEU) (2003) *A Better Education for Children in Care*, London: SEU.

Statham, J., Candappa, M., Simon, A. and Owen, C. (2002) *Trends in Care: Exploring Reasons for the Increase in Children Looked After by Local Authorities*, London: University of London Institute of Education.

Whittaker, D., Archer, L. and Hicks, L. (1998) *Working in Children's Homes: Challenges and Complexities*, Chichester: Wiley.

The impact of HIV/AIDS: Education as a window of hope for the future?

10 Gabriella Torstensson and Mark Brundrett

Chapter Outline

Introduction

The disease which has come to be known as *Human Immunodeficiency Virus* or *Acquired Immune Deficiency Syndrome* (HIV/AIDS) first emerged in the early 1980s. While HIV refers to the virus that is transmitted mainly, but not exclusively, through unprotected sexual contact, AIDS is the advanced form of the condition which follows infection and is characterized by a severe breakdown of the body's ability to fight disease. HIV/AIDS now constitutes a global pandemic which has impacted on individuals, families and national and regional economies through the stress it places on key social systems. Nowhere has this impact been greater than in sub-Saharan Africa where a number of factors have elided to create a crisis of previously unimagined proportions.

This chapter focuses on the effects of HIV/AIDS on education in Southern Africa and is based on a study of several countries in the region, placing particular emphasis on the situation that prevails in Botswana. A number of key contentions are presented to the reader which include the following:

- HIV/AIDS has impacted all areas of social life in the region including and especially education
- Educational institutions have been viewed as central to ameliorating the effects of the pandemic
- An essentially Western notion of school effectiveness has been artificially imposed on the educational approaches employed in the fight against the disease
- It is open to question whether more nuanced and local solutions might not be more effective in addressing the effects of HIV/AIDS.

Challenging conventional wisdom

In essence, the chapter problematizes some of the conventional wisdom in response to the immense dislocation caused by HIV/AIDS and suggests that other, more culturally nuanced, approaches may actually be more beneficial. In so doing, the writers are conscious that when faced with the breadth of the problem of HIV/AIDS it is easy, almost essential, to adopt a clinical perspective that distances the academic/reader from the enormity of human distress and social dysfunction that has followed the disease. However, we must remember that HIV/AIDS has become an intensely personal tragedy faced daily by many thousands, indeed millions, of people in Africa and around the world. Thus, education has a central role to play in limiting the spread of the disease and its wider societal effects. The analysis presented here is structured around an examination of the emergence of the disease followed by an exploration of the impact of HIV/AIDS at the twin-levels of pupil and classroom. Finally, we present an exposition of the ways in which education can be used to construct a window of hope for the future.

Useful Websites

Avert International AIDS charity working with children	www.avert.org/children.htm
SOS Children's villages Major charity working with aids orphans in Southern Africa	www.soschildrensvillages.org.uk/children-charity.htm/
AIDS Map Map of the extent of the AIDS pandemic	www.aidsmap.com/en/news/45E5AF11-7AC0-470A-9256-08598D55784B.asp
Aidsportal Website that contains a great deal of information on AIDS	www.aidsportal.org/Article_Details.aspx?ID=7876

The emergence of HIV/AIDS and the examination of the associated educational issues through school effectiveness approaches

Since HIV/AIDS was first discovered in 1981, infection rates have soared from just a few cases to approximately 39.5 million in 2006, with 4.5 million new infections in that year (UNAIDS, 2006). Sub-Saharan Africa which is hardest hit, and hosts 63 per cent of all AIDS infected people globally, has its epicentre in Southern Africa. Here, infection rates currently stand at 33.4 per cent in Botswana (Seipore, 2006), 30.2 per cent in South Africa (Department of Health, South Africa, 2006), 24 per cent in Zimbabwe (UNAIDS, 2005) and 10 to 25 per cent in Zambia (Ministry of Health, 2005). For many young children of primary age, parents' (typically aged 30 to 35) infection rates continue to escalate (Seipore, 2006), leaving many children bereaved as orphans – (13.2 million worldwide between 1992 and 2001). By 2005, sub-Saharan Africa had 12 million orphans, with 57,964 of them living in Botswana (NACA, 2005). Already in the late 1990s, Zambia had more than 130,000 child headed families, and 860,000 South African children had become teacherless (Coombe, 2001). While early predicative studies suggest that AIDS will impact the supply, demand and financial resources available to education (in terms of influencing educational processes and products within schools (Kelly, 1999)), later studies indicate that early reports had grossly overestimated the impact of AIDS. This is because teacher death and orphan ratios remain lower than predicted, suggesting various education systems are able to cope with increasing mortality rates (Bennell, 2005). However, this fact and the argument that the AIDS pandemic has stagnated, as new infection rates now align with death rates (UNAIDS, 2006), does not adequately account for the loss of human life. It does not take into consideration, for example, lost potential or the benefit that people may have contributed to society had they remained alive. Further, such studies collectively fail to reflect the qualitative impact that AIDS is having upon pupils and the classroom, as they frequently gloss over factors that correlate positively with levels of academic achievement and pupils' learning prospects in the long term.

HIV/AIDS education programmes

The combined effort of numerous governments, charities and aid organizations has led to the development of HIV/AIDS education programmes, the establishment of new testing centres and numerous condom distribution programmes. These have been set up in order to mitigate the impact and trend of widespread infection. While these efforts have played a critical role in raising the level of awareness about AIDS, infection rates still continue to rise in all continents of the world (UNAIDS, 2006). Indeed, when certain high-achieving students with scholarships to universities abroad return home in coffins, and where the only real long-term solution lies in large-scale behavioural change, it is questionable whether a system of education in which the yardstick of quality is measured via academic test scores in maths and literacy, is in any way sufficient to address the problem. Thus, we argue that in view of the impending crisis of illness and disease and in order to stem the spread of infection, it is not nearly enough to ensure that information regarding AIDS and appropriate forms of protection are integrated within the curriculum.

In a swiftly changing, market-driven and increasingly globalized world, in which economic competitiveness between nations continues to influence educational policy and practice, the so-called developing region of Southern Africa is unable to escape the pervasive trends of performativity. Within education this has led to a growing need for regular feedback regarding the status of pupils' attainment at different levels of the system, and data is often used to inform and modify practice, as well as rankings in international league tables. School effectiveness research (SER), which, through statistical means, tries to identify and measure universal process variables that correlate positively with academic tests scores of basic skills in maths and language, after contextual factors have been controlled, has often been used as a tool to obtain comparative data.

School effectiveness research

SER models, with a dominant perspective that views schooling as a 'black box' for experimentation and empirical analysis, have, arguably, led to a greater understanding of the many factors influencing pupils' attainment at different levels of schooling. However, while the limited focus on a small number of measurable outcomes, can enhance the transferability and comparison between nations, Fidler (2001) argues that this narrow focus has detracted attention away from the broader curriculum, higher order learning and moral and social aspects of learning. Moreover, taking the emphasis on measurable outcomes as *de facto*, the paradigm has been challenged for its conservative orientation and failure to engage in the debate about important educational and human values and goals that are required in a changing society and globalizing world (Slee et al., 1998). Nevertheless, policy makers and inspectorate systems in different countries have used both methods and findings from SER as a vehicle for macro-political change and to hold schools accountable, compare schools across national and cultural borders and as benchmarks to improve schools.

Southern Africa

In the context of Southern Africa and with specific reference to the impact of HIV/AIDS, school effectiveness approaches have impinged on, and helped to frame, the educational response to the developing crisis since many national and international agencies have moulded their response around the notion of making intervention strategies and, crucially, funding contingent upon comparatively easily measurable outcomes. In the context of the overarching hegemonic influence of SER approaches such strategies are understandable and are designed to ensure both impact and accountability. However, Hamilton (1998) and Ball (1998) argue that the use of such SER strategies may, in many instances, lead to an overemphasis on short-term thinking and superficial solutions in the form 'best-fit-all D-I-Y' school improvement packages. Effectiveness processes are also increasingly migrating across national borders through international educational aid packages to developing countries without taking into account the local context. However, not only may the aim of universality at the process level be questionable between countries where schools are challenged by contextual factors such as war, poverty, inequalities and discrimination, but the appropriateness of using universal findings to secure quick measurable results, in contexts such as a growing AIDS pandemic (where long term, large scale behaviour change may be the only solution to turn the trend around), may also be debatable.

The succeeding sections of this chapter unpack some of the ways in which these dominant transnational approaches to intervention, dependant as they are on a limited number of measurable outcomes, may ignore important contextual factors with an inevitable impact on the efficacy of the relevant initiatives.

The impact of HIV/AIDS on pupils

In exploring pupils' learning from a school effectiveness perspective, pupils' attainment can be interpreted as a 'function of the time actually spent divided by the time actually needed by a student' (Creemers et al., 2000: 283). Attainments and learning are thus influenced by factors such as pupils' aptitude, ability to understand, perseverance, motivation, opportunity, quality of instruction and the time available to learn (Caroll, 1963). In areas with high HIV/AIDS prevalence, the impact of AIDS is not only affecting children's home and family life, but also their opportunities to learn. Unlike many studies which have primarily focused on AIDS orphans, findings from this study indicate that children are severely affected by AIDS from the day they begin to suspect their parents may be ill.

Parents

As parents become unwell, the child's home-life becomes affected by illness, sadness, fears and anxieties. Parents' ability to work and care for the family is reduced and gradually the family income is depleted. The responsibility of caring for the household, sick parents, younger siblings and the economy often falls upon the shoulders of older children. As parental sickness patterns become more severe and unstable, it is often the case that opportunities for pupils to consider and plan their future become more limited; so much so that some lives can become completely dominated by the ongoing needs of the parents' illness. The effects are profound: children's psycho-emotional well-being is severely impaired and in many cases the psychological impact of such chronic illness is as great, if not greater than, parental death itself. Vulnerable children typically become withdrawn, anxious, isolated, depressed and irrepressibly tearful, with many fearing the worst of an AIDS related stigma and/or further social isolation.

AIDS orphans

While Meinthes (2004) has suggested that being an AIDS orphan is in many ways no different from any situation in which children are brought up by relatives while parents work away from home, or indeed perhaps brought up in relatively 'poor' families, elsewhere it has been argued that:

> without exception, children orphaned by AIDS are marginalised, stigmatised, malnourished, uneducated and psychologically damaged...Many deal with trauma, face the most dangerous threats and have least protection. And because of this they are likely to become HIV/AIDS positive. (UNICEF, 2001: 1)

Studies in Southern Africa have shown that the plight of orphans – that is, their ability to recover from the immediate bereavement of one or both parents, to feel settled in a new home and/or continue with their schooling – is largely dependent upon the quality and type of care received, which can vary between relatives (grandparents, uncles and aunts) and across rural and urban areas. Guest (2001) and Matshalaga (2004), for example, found that orphans in Zimbabwe and Zambia, who were cared for by uncles and aunts, were financially better off and more likely to continue schooling than those cared for by grandparents. However, while the latter were more likely to suffer economic hardship, receive less discipline and active encouragement to continue schooling, it is reported that they often felt more loved and cared for. In Botswana, many children felt that grandparents provided a level of greater care than say, uncles and aunts. For example, one 12-year-old attending an urban school in Botswana described how two of her friends who had lost their mother were no longer welcome in their father's house. Although the aunt initially took care of them, the children did not feel welcome, nor did they feel they were treated equally. For many of the children in the study in Botswana, grandparents were often regarded as security for future well-being – in the event that anything should happen to their parents. Unfortunately, the increasing number of orphans relative to grandparents, and glaring disparity between orphaned children and income generating adults, means that this source of security and support can all too easily be exceeded and overrun.

Social and educational contexts

In order to counteract the escalating financial implications of supporting the orphans of relatives, the government of Botswana now provides a food basket (or the equivalent in money) and free secondary education for every registered orphan. While case studies in Zimbabwe and Zambia found that many boys had to drop out from school in order to substitute the family income, and the education of many girls became more random as they looked after sick family members and younger siblings (Guest, 2001; Matshalaga, 2004), in Botswana most boys and girls were able to remain in school. Even so, in some cases children's ability to keep up with school work was severely impeded by the need to look after other orphaned children and sick members of the family. An inherent lack of money could also mean that some children were not able to buy school uniforms, pay their fees or purchase learning items. However, teachers and children in Botswana noted that children who were well cared for in their new homes, slowly regained a sense of 'self'. While those less well settled often exhibited more volatile behaviour, along with a discernible lack of hope for the future and purpose in life. Children described how orphans were often stigmatized within their communities, called names and unduly blamed for their parents' death. Schools, on the other hand, were often described as 'safe havens'.

Fear

Although the impact of AIDS is clearly worse for children with immediate experience of the illness and parental death, an overwhelming majority of children (in the Botswanan study) were said to live in constant fear. This was the case regardless of the level of experience of AIDS within the family and/or community; in fact, many feared, at some point, their parents might fall ill and eventually die. Teachers described how children had a tendency to show signs of trauma and distress at the point when parents began to suffer with common colds, often misrecognized as the onset of AIDS. For a whole range of reasons, children also feared the potential to contract the virus: being pressured into having sex; being raped; caring for younger siblings with HIV; through fights; through becoming drunk and losing the ability to negotiate safe sex. Such anxieties around infection are exacerbated by the stigma surrounding AIDS, a taboo where many children feel unable to disclose their worries and fears, the escalation of which is often based on incorrect knowledge and multiple erroneous assumptions. While knowledge of AIDS is vital in order for children to protect themselves against the virus, incorrect forms of knowledge or simply the lack of ability to act, can lead to even greater anxiety and provoke further risky behaviour as a means to comfort stress.

The AIDS pandemic

The scale and reach of the AIDS pandemic, featured strongly in the discourse of children's perceptions of the future, regardless of their actual level of experience of AIDS or whether, in fact, they held positive or negative views. Their descriptions ranged from 'Botswana will be a beautiful country with big cities and houses with electricity' to 'Botswana will be finished because of this killer disease' (Torstensson, 2007: 157). Although, in total, 31 per cent of children had a positive perception of the future – their own and Botswana's – based on the optimistic view of AIDS being eradicated, 36 per cent had an almost apocalyptic perspective, where AIDS had destroyed families, communities and the entire country, with children being left to fend for themselves. A proportion of 16 per cent wished for a better future, while another 16 per cent perceived two possible scenarios: positive and negative. The positive scenario was contingent on the discovery of a cure for AIDS or a belief in the possibility of radical change in people's behaviour. While a positive vision of the future can be linked to the development of various coping strategies, the study found that children in possession of a 'wishful view' or dual perception of the future, had a broader range of strategies to protect themselves, and were thus more inclined to take an active role in turning the trend around. Many of the children with a positive perception believed that either the government or medical profession would eventually invent a cure. A number of children in rural areas, where the stigma and taboo of AIDS was relatively strong, had not been able to relate what they had learnt about AIDS in school with what was happening in their community. Moreover, the majority of children in possession of a negative perspective of the future could not recognize or count upon any strategies to protect themselves. Nor, for that matter, did they feel optimistic about turning the trend around. Similarly, many orphaned children had no strategies to protect themselves. Thus, although children in general had a very good knowledge of AIDS, surprisingly many felt that the solution lie elsewhere in external sources, such as a medical cure or government support, as opposed to modifying their own and others' actual behaviour.

Misconception of the issues

Consequently, while many academic studies and mass media reports have contributed to the global misconception that AIDS only affects children with more direct experience of the illness, this study presents a decidedly more complex picture. We suggest that the constituent parts of the lives of all children – comprising levels of motivation, behaviour, perceptions of self and sense of the future – are profoundly impacted by the AIDS pandemic. As such, AIDS not only serves to impair the range of pupil level factors that correlate positively with academic outcomes, it also inhibits those that contribute towards, and further support, pupils in making healthy life choices and playing an active role in transforming the negative trend.

The impact of HIV/AIDS in the classroom

Where an increasing proportion of children's parents are dying, the well-being of the next generation, to a very large degree, can be said to rest on teachers' shoulders. However, when

20 per cent of all Zambia's teachers (Kelly, 1999), 12 per cent of South African teachers (ABT Associates, 2001) and 30 per cent of Malawian teachers (UNICEF, 1999), were reported in 1996 to be already infected (i.e. HIV positive), this seems more than a little optimistic. While statistically teacher death rates in schools remain relatively low, it must be noted that prior to death a teacher will typically suffer a whole range of AIDS related illnesses and emotional conditions, which inevitably impact on classroom attendance, as well as their ability to teach effectively.

Activity

1. What do you consider the long-term impact of HIV/AIDS will have on the social structures of Southern Africa? What are the responsibilities of the rich Western nations?

Teacher perceptions

In reviewing teachers' perceptions of the impact of AIDS upon their lives and teaching careers, three distinct phases seemed to emerge. The first phase in the period leading up to being tested and awaiting results was described as being filled with fears and anxieties. For some this led to outright avoidance, in which further delays were created in being tested and receiving results. In some cases, this produced symptoms of acute withdrawal and depression. Indeed, there were cases in which some people left it so late that the Antiretroviral Treatment (ART) had no effect whatsoever.

The second phase

In the second phase, when teachers had been informed they were HIV positive, many exhibited symptoms of withdrawal, depression and a loss of hope. One headteacher in a rural school in Botswana described how one of her best colleagues, who upon discovering she was HIV positive was initially absent for weeks after receiving the results. On return, her character was reported to have completely changed; that is, from being a positive and effective teacher she had lost all energy and purpose in life (and in teaching), and was often seen walking around the school with a glazed expression. It transpired that this teacher had been counselled for some time before she actively sought treatment; however, when she finally received ART it was too late.

The third phase

While many teachers, in the third phase of progression, had begun to receive ART in time to enable a return to relatively normal health after three to six months of treatment, typically headteachers described how their colleagues' perceptions of self and their outlook on life had become openly pessimistic, leading to significantly reduced energy levels. For a number of Botswanan teachers determined not to access free ART for fear of stigmatization – or otherwise losing status within their family and community – and for teachers in other countries where ART is not free or readily available, the third phase was often punctuated with recurring AIDS related illnesses, resulting in frequent absenteeism. Regardless, most of the teachers interviewed described how they lived in constant fear that they, their partners or family would eventually test positive, become sick and die. Both children and teachers felt that AIDS had brought a level of depression over the country, which caused people to feel unsettled and worry about their future, as well as that of their community and nation. While the overall level of mortality and increasing number of HIV positive teachers within Botswanan schools was lower than expected, the impact of ill health on attendance was regarded as a real problem. For example, there was evidence that the seriously ill were recorded absent for weeks at a time, while less severe cases were registered absent a few days every fortnight. In the later stages of advanced illness, sickness records showed that teachers were absent for between 40 and 60 days per term. However, increased levels of absenteeism were shown not only to relate to those with HIV, but also those caring for sick family members, sick relatives and/or those attending funerals. This was seen to have a profound effect on pupil learning. For example, Das et al. (2004) found that similar sickness levels in Zambia led to a significant decline in learning (down 20 to 30 per cent) over a period of one year. The impact of this was more severe in rural and remote areas, where access to treatment and support was less readily available and teachers would need to travel, sometimes up to two days, to reach a hospital.

Supply teachers

In many countries in the West, a supply teacher can easily be hired in the morning when a colleague is absent. However in many schools in Africa, where teachers are in short supply or cover arrangements are organized centrally, groups will have to be divided between remaining classes. In Botswana, where the teacher–pupil ratio is approximately 25–30:1, this could mean that teachers in a two-form-entry school would have to teach up to 60 pupils in one classroom. In Zambia, where class sizes are even larger, the teacher ratio can reach up to 80 or 90 students when classes are doubled in some small schools. This not only affects a teacher's ability to support individuals or groups of students – in terms of keeping up with planning and marking, differentiating lesson content, and monitoring approaches to teaching and learning – but it forces a situation in which explorative methodologies are often reduced to whole class lecturing and/or a process of copying work. A lack of interaction in certain subjects, which rely upon group work, can sometimes lead to students falling behind. Moreover, in cases where teachers are no longer adequately fit to teach more practical subjects like home economics, agriculture and sport, such subjects tend to be taught less frequently or, at best, are less well taught.

The classroom environment

Aside from the numerous critical factors that relate to the context of the pupil, there are multiple complexities pertaining to the classroom environment. Caroll (1963), for example, suggests that pupils' attainment is affected by factors of grouping, planning and assessment, teacher behaviour and the effective use of resources and curriculum. However, in the context of AIDS the effectiveness of such pedagogical factors is also attenuated. Although many pupils saw school as a safe haven where they could be free from stigma and forget their sorrows, teachers nonetheless noted how pupils' fears, anxieties, sadness and depression served to influence their ability to focus upon learning. Pupils also noted how peers with sick parents easily became upset and tearful, lonely and absent minded, and effectively struggled to learn in school.

School attendance

As parental illness became worse so too did pupils' school attendance, along with their ability to keep up with assignments and school work. Children's grades began to drop from above average to well below average and from an 'A' to a 'C', when parents became ill or worse, died. This reduction was especially marked if it was the mother who was ill. However, for those children who settled well into their new homes following the untimely death of a parent, their grades gradually began to improve again. Those less fortunate continued to sustain low grades or a level of performance that continued to drop. The cumulative impact of at least five to eight months of ineffective learning following parental death, coupled with the estimated reduction in the quality of teaching and learning (Das et al., 2004) – due to teacher's ill health in the advanced stages of disease – can mean a considerable loss in learning for all children, but especially those orphaned and vulnerable children taught by sick teachers. AIDS related fears also affected levels of pupil motivation, with many children feeling helpless and confused, struggling to see a way to protect themselves and reverse the trend.

Stigma and isolation

While in some countries in Southern Africa the stigma of AIDS is leading to the widespread isolation and exclusion of many groups from society, children in Botswana showed great courage and willingness to support those affected and in pain. This included looking after and caring for orphans and helping out other children with their homework. Similarly, teachers literally spent hours supporting colleagues who had fallen ill and preparing remedial work for children, including visiting the carers of those for whom regular school attendance had significantly dropped. In contrast with studies carried out in other Southern African countries, which have suggested that teachers were fearful of those who were sick and thus sought ways to avoid them, or otherwise felt that it was not their responsibility to teach children about HIV/AIDS (Visser, 2004), all teachers in this study exhibited a positive attitude towards sufferers and felt it was their duty to support and teach children about AIDS.

Schools as a vehicle for turning around the effects of HIV/AIDS

In order for schools to become a vehicle for change in the process of responding to the HIV/AIDS pandemic, Kelly (1999) has suggested that they first need to ensure they have sufficient knowledge and understanding of the issues, along with the ability to cope with the impact of the illness upon their pupils. This requires that teachers have sufficient knowledge of AIDS, are regularly tested and, in the Botswanan case, willing to access and benefit from the availability of free ART. In the absence of a medical cure, it is imperative that this knowledge leads to behaviour change. Though many HIV prevention and mitigation strategies work on the assumption that knowledge of AIDS and its transmission automatically leads to a positive change in behaviour, this and other studies have shown that this is not the case (ABT Associates, 2002; BIDPA, 2003; Visser, 2004). Cultural values and beliefs, attitudes relating to gender and equality, perceptions of responsibility towards self and others and the ability to analyse and recognize temporal patterns – in order to develop a vision for the future – are collectively related to the individual's ability to convert knowledge about AIDS into responsible behaviour and safe practice.

Strategies for change

Many mitigation strategies have been based on short-term measurable goals that are often focused on fairly superficial aims, such as delivering AIDS education packages and/or distributing condoms. However, large-scale changes in behaviour and cultural practice require long-term strategies that touch the roots of the problem rather than simply seeking to address the symptoms of AIDS. Findings from this study support Delors et al.'s (1996) notion, and the UN's argument that schools in the twenty-first century must work to challenge the hegemony of academic subjects, in order to place equal value on the domains: 'Learning to know', 'Learning to do', 'Learning to be' and 'Learning to live together'. As many of the values and attitudes that influence behaviour are already developed by the age of 10, children in primary schools, in addition to learning through traditional academic subjects, also need to be exposed to opportunities to develop skills in lateral thinking, curiosity, critical questioning, and the process of engaging analytically with both practical and theoretical forms of knowledge, using a range of conceptual tools. Children need to develop a more sophisticated understanding of the operation and intricacies of interdependence, of patterns and systems in nature, of traditional and modern forms of governance and, fundamentality, of humanity in order to understand how contemporary issues integrate with radical solutions. This presupposes a learning pedagogy in which children are much more active in the process of acquiring knowledge and understanding, both in terms of undertaking projects inside and outside school, but also in seizing opportunities to become involved in debates and classroom discussions, along with research, drama and problem solving activities. Such learning opportunities, linked to a futures perspective, in which temporal considerations (past, present and future) are related to the roles and responsibilities of people working collectively within their communities, would serve to enhance their ability to act as agents of social change.

Conclusion

It is clear that HIV/AIDS is no longer a health problem that affects only a small minority of people suffering with the disease or those otherwise orphaned by the sweeping pandemic. The profound and debilitating impact of AIDS is now universally experienced across all levels of schooling and society in the Southern African region. Despite this fact, we argue that the pervasive influence of school effectiveness research, employed as a vehicle for macro-political and educational change, has tended to focus too narrowly on the development of traditional academic aims and performance measurement. This has come at the expense of articulating a more holistic and nuanced programme of education, in order to meet the needs of communities where HIV/AIDS is highly prevalent and thus a real problem.

Activity

1. Using the web as a research tool, what are the arguments that HIV/AIDS is a disease of poverty above all else?

The complexity and enduring nature of this problem, we argue requires broad-ranging and integrated solutions at all levels of the education system. Moreover, in the absence of a medical cure or any firm evidence that imputed levels of knowledge have impacted positively on behaviour, schools must be active in educating pupils to protect themselves. That is, active in terms of challenging issues that lie at the very core of the problem and at the heart of a critical pedagogy that seeks to empower and bring about social transformation and change. Only then can pupils begin to play a more active role in redefining what counts as quality within education, beyond the narrow confines of an academic curriculum. While recognizing that the global dominance of SER strategies, and understandable demand of accountability for funding through measurable outcomes, may make these ideas contentious and problematic for government already struggling to cope with problems of unprecedented proportions, we argue that radical change requires radical action.

Thus, if communities are to respond to the countless stories of personal tragedy associated with HIV/AIDS – stories that extend far and beyond the performative metric of simple numeric analysis – schools, teachers and pupils have no alternative but to be proactive. It is worth noting that in the very different context of the pre HIV/AIDS era, Bernstein (1968) argued that schools cannot compensate for society. In the new and immeasurably more challenging situation presented by the HIV/AIDS pandemic in Southern Africa, we ask the question: if schools do not take on the task of attempting to mitigate societal problems, who will?

Key Points

- HIV/AIDS emerged in the 1980s and is primarily, though not exclusively, a sexually transmitted disease
- HIV is now at the levels of a pandemic in parts of the world, especially Southern Africa
- Education has been identified by governments, charities and various NGOs as one of the key methods of ameliorating the effects of the pandemic
- Education is viewed as the most effective way to change existing behaviour patterns that have led to the massive spread of the disease
- However, Western approaches to education, especially the school effectiveness approach have been imposed on the countries of Southern Africa
- Evidence shows that a more culturally sensitive approach based on the cultures and traditions of the impacted communities may be more effective
- HIV/AIDS is having a major impact on children regardless of whether they are orphans
- HIV/AIDS is impacting on family structures through the death of parents
- HIV/AIDS is impacting on the teaching profession, at least through the death rate.
- The problem with the adopted educational approach is that there is a narrow academic focus and emphasis on performance measurement, which has come at the expense of articulating a more holistic and nuanced programme of education.

Further Reading

Coombe, C. (2001) *HIV/AIDS and Trauma among Learners*, Pretoria: National Union of educators.

Slee, R., Weiner, G. and Tomlinson, S. (eds) (1998) *School Effectiveness for Whom?* London: Falmer Press.

The United Nations Children's Fund (UNICEF) (1999) *The Progress of Nations*, New York: UNICEF.

References

ABT Associates (2001) *Impact of HIV/Aids on the South African Education Sector: Summary*, Johannesburg: ABT Associates.

ABT Associates (2002) *Impact of HIV/Aids on the Botswana Education Sector: Summary*, Gaborone: ABT Associates and Botswana Ministry of Education.

Ball, S. (1998) 'Educational studies, policy, entrepreneurship and social theory', in R. Slee, G. Weiner and S. Tomlinson (eds), *School Effectiveness for Whom? Challenges to the School Effectiveness and School Improvement Movements*, Bristol: Falmer Press.

Bennell, P. (2005) 'The impact of AIDS epidemic on the schooling of orphans and other directly affected children in sub-Saharan Africa', *Journal of Development Studies*, 41 (3): 467–88.

Bernstein, B. (1968) 'Education cannot compensate for society', *New Society*, 387: 334–7.

Botswana Institute for Development Policy Analysis (BIDPA) (2003) *Knowledge, Attitudes and Practices of Teachers and Students on HIV and AIDS – Baseline Study Report*, Gaborone: BIDPA.

Caroll, J. B. (1963) 'A model of school learning', *Teacher College Record*, 64 (8): 723–33.

Coombe, C. (2001) *HIV/AIDS and Trauma among Learners*, Pretoria: National Union of educators.

Creemers, B., Sheerens, J. and Reynolds, D. (2000) 'Theory development in school effectiveness research', in C. Teddlie and D. Reynolds (eds), *International Handbook of School Effectiveness Research*, Lewes: Falmer Press.

Das, J., Dercon, S., Habyarimana, J. and Krishnan, P. (2004) *Teacher Shocks and Students Learning: Evidence from Zambia*; CSAE WPS/2004–26, World Bank/DfID.

Delors, J., Mufti, I. A., Amagi, I., Carneiro, R., Chung, F., Geremek, B., Gorham, W., Kornhauser, A., Manley, M., Quero, M. P., Savane, M. A., Singh, K., Stavenhagen, R., Won Suhr, M. and Nanzhoa, Z. (1996) *Learning: The Treasure Within*, Paris: UNESCO.

Department of Health, South Africa (2006) *National HIV and Syphilis Antenatal Prevalence Survey, South Africa 2005*, Pretoria: Department of Health South Africa.

Fidler, B. (2001) 'A structural critique of school effectiveness and school improvement', in A. Harris and N. Bennett (eds), *School Effectiveness and School Improvement: Alternative Perspectives*, London: Continuum.

Guest, E. (2001) *Children of AIDS: Africa's Orphan Crisis*, Scottsville: University of Natal Press.

Hamilton, D. (1998) 'The idols of the Market Place', in R. Slee, G. Weiner and S. Tomlison (eds), *School Effectiveness for Whom? Challenges to the School Effectiveness and School Improvement Movements*, Bristol: Falmer Press.

Kelly, M. (1999) *The Impact of HIV/AIDS on Schooling in Zambia*, paper presented at XIth International Conference of AIDS and STDD in Africa; Lusaka, Zambia, 12–16 September 1999.

Matshalaga, N. (2004) *Grandmothers and Orphan Care in Zimbabwe*, Harare: SAfAIDS.

Meinthes, H. (2004) 'Spinning the epidemic: the making of mythology of orphanhood in the context of AIDS', paper presented at symposium *Life and Death in the Time of AIDS: The Southern African Experience*, Wits University, Johannesburg, South Africa, October, 2004.

Ministry of Health, Zambia (2005) *Zambia Antenatal Sentinel Surveillance Report 1994–2004*, Lusaka: Ministry of Health, Zambia.

National AIDS Coordinating Agency (NACA) (2005) *Botswana HIV/AIDS Response Information Management System January to March*, Report, Gaborone: Ministry of State President.

Seipore, K. M. D. (2006) *Trends of HIV Prevalence in Botswana; Department of HIV/AIDS Prevention and Care*. Gaborone: Ministry of Health, Botswana.

Slee, R., Weiner, G. and Tomlinson, S. (eds) (1998) *School Effectiveness for Whom?*, London: Falmer Press.

Torstensson, G. (2007) 'Managing the impact of HIV/Aids in Botswana's education system: redefining effective teaching and learning in the context of AIDS', Leicester University: Unpublished doctoral thesis.

The Joint United Nations Programme on HIV/AIDS (UNAIDS) (2005) *Evidence for HIV Decline in Zimbabwe: A Comprehensive Review of Epidemiological Data*, November 2006, Geneva: UNAIDS.

The Joint United Nations Programme on HIV/AIDS (UNAIDS), WHO (2006) *AIDS Epidemic Update*, December 2006.

The United Nations Children's Fund (UNICEF) (1999) *The Progress of Nations*, New York: UNICEF.

The United Nations Children's Fund (UNICEF) (2001) *UNICEF Calls Global Response to Children Orphaned by AIDS Grossly Inadequate*, Press release, Windhoek, Namibia.

Visser, M. (2004) *The Impact of Individual Differences on the Willingness of Teachers in Mozambique to Communicate about HIV/AIDS in Schools and Communities*, Florida State University: Unpublished doctoral thesis.

11 No Child Left Behind, really?

David Hursh

Introduction

The No Child Left Behind Act (NCLB) represents the largest federal intervention into local education policy in the history of the US. Historically, teaching, curriculum and assessment decisions have been made by schools or school districts (the community level administrative unit) and not at the state or federal levels. However, NCLB passed with large majorities in both the Senate (87-10) and the House (381-41), and was signed into law by President Bush on 8 January 2002.

I begin this chapter by describing some of the central features of NCLB, particularly focusing on those aspects that made it attractive both to Democrats and Republicans. However, I also situate the Act within the rise of neo-liberal policies that focus on transforming governmental agencies through privatization and conversion to markets. This additional aspect raises the question of whether some of those supporting NCLB intended not to improve public education but to disparage it and push for its privatization.

I then turn to evaluating the effects of NCLB and provide evidence that the reforms have resulted in decreased learning and undermined educational and societal efforts that would contribute to improved student learning. Therefore, I conclude this chapter with recommendations for educational and social policies that would improve student learning.

No Child Left Behind

The NCLB Act affects almost every aspect of education at the elementary and secondary levels, including additional testing and curriculum requirements for preschools, limiting federally funded educational research to quantitative studies with control groups, and requiring that secondary schools provide military recruiters with the students' names and contract information – (see *No Child Left Behind: A Parents' Guide* (2003) for an overview of NCLB). However, in this chapter, I will focus on the standardized testing requirements, and the penalties that schools and school districts face for not demonstrating Adequate Yearly Progress (AYP) on the exams.

Testing requirements

The central and most discussed feature of NCLB is its testing requirements and the potential consequences for schools and school districts. Previous to NCLB, most states had implemented standardized testing requirements in a few subjects and grades, typically in the core subjects at the end of the primary and intermediate grades. NCLB imposed the additional requirement that students be tested in reading (not literacy), mathematics and science in grades 3 through 8 (typically ages 8 to 13). In addition, these subjects were to be assessed once during the secondary years. Since most states had their own additional testing requirements in other subjects, students may end up taking numerous exams each year. In New York, for example, students confront a minimum of 33 standardized exams over 10 years. Some of these exams are administered over two school days.

NCLB requires that students' test scores be presented both in an aggregated and disaggregated format, with separate scores provided for groups of a minimum size (typically 30 students) by gender, race and ethnicity, English as a Second Language learners, and students with disabilities. These disaggregated scores are compared to state minimum requirements for achieving AYP. To avoid sanctions, every disaggregated subgroup must meet these minimum requirements.

Moreover, AYP does not measure, as the name implies, whether a school is making annual yearly progress, but measures whether a school is meeting a minimum threshold of students passing the exams that gradually increases from the year NCLB was implemented until 2014. At which point, all students, regardless of ability, whether they have only arrived in the US and speak little or no English or have a significant disability, will be required to pass every test, to be 'proficient'.

Disaggregating test scores and evaluating schools based on whether they meet a minimum threshold increases the chances that urban schools will be judged to be 'failing'. Because urban schools in the US typically have both a more diverse student body composed of multiple races and ethnicities and have a higher percentage of students living in poverty, they are more likely to be judged to be failing. Because they are more diverse, they may have dozens of racial and ethnic groups assessed by gender, race and disability, therefore exponentially increasing the odds that one group will fail to meet the threshold and cause the whole school to be found as failing.

Family status and pupil achievement

As test scores strongly correlate with a student's family income; a school's score is more likely to reflect their students' average family income than the quality of the teaching or the curriculum. Therefore, by evaluating schools, based on whether their test scores meet a minimum threshold rather than on whether they are actually improving, serves to disadvantage schools that are already behind. For example, a school with already high passing rates will continue to be considered passing as long as their scores exceed the threshold, even if their scores fall. Similarly, schools that begin with initially low test scores may be considered failing even if they significantly improve their test scores, as long as those scores remain below the threshold. Therefore, achieving AYP may have nothing to do with whether a school's test scores rise or fall; achieving AYP depends only on exceeding the minimum threshold, which advantages middle and upper-class schools.

Failing schools

As a result, the largest percentage of failing schools is in poor, urban school districts. For example, in New York almost all (83 per cent) of the failing schools are located in the big five urban districts: New York City, Buffalo, Rochester, Syracuse and Yonkers. Most of the remaining failing schools can be found in smaller urban districts. The failure rate among schools in large urban districts is high, particularly at the middle school level. In Rochester (NY), for example, all the middle schools failed, which led the superintendent to fold all the middle schools into grade 7–12 schools, thus essentially creating 'new' schools, temporarily averting penalties for failing to meet AYP.

Failing to achieve AYP has real consequences. If schools do not make adequate yearly progress for two consecutive years, they must be identified as schools 'in need of improvement'. Students in those schools must be given the option of transferring to another public school (U.S. Department of Education, 2003a: 6). Additional requirements are imposed for each successive year that a school fails to meet adequate yearly progress goals. These include no longer providing students with supplemental tutoring, after-school programs, remedial classes or summer school, but having those services provided by private, often less effective, organizations, replacing the school staff, implementing a new curriculum, 'decreasing management authority, appointing an outside expert to advise the school, extending the school day or year, or reorganizing the school internally'. Schools failing for five consecutive years must either reopen as a charter school, replace all or most of the school staff who are relevant to the failure to make adequate yearly progress, or turn over the operations either to the state or to 'a private company with a demonstrated record of effectiveness' (6–8). Many of the 'remedies,' such as tutoring, remedial classes and replacing the administration, provide opportunities for private corporations to profit from public funding.

The rationale for NCLB

In promoting NCLB, the Bush administration, like those who previously pushed for high-stakes testing at the state level (Hursh, 2005, 2007a, 2007b, 2008), argued that globalization requires increased efficiency, accountability, fairness and equality. President Bush, for example, recently touted the need for and success of NCLB claiming:

> NCLB is an important way to make sure America remains competitive in the 21st century. We're living in a global world. See, the education system must compete with education systems in China and India. If we fail to give our students the skills necessary to compete in the world in the 21st century, the jobs will go elsewhere. (U.S. Department of Education, 2006b: 2)

NCLB, then, is touted as a response to global competition, in which the US is falling behind. Rodney Paige (Bush's first secretary of education) described how NCLB will increase our educational efficiency, ensure that all children will learn, and close the achievement gap between the US and other countries. Paige, in response to an Organization of Economic and Co-operative Development report, describes education as an economic investment:

> This report documents how little we receive for our national investment. This report also reminds us that we are battling two achievement gaps. One is between those who are being served well by our system and those being left behind. The other is between the U.S. and many of our higher achieving friends around the world. By closing the first gap, we will close the second. (Education Review, 2003)

Useful Websites

No Child Left Behind official website — www.ed.gov/nclb/landing.jhtml

Rethinking schools Online
Radical educational journal based in North America — www.rethinkingschools.org/special_reports/bushplan/index.shtml

Journal of Critical Education Policies
Left leaning e-journal – articles are free — www.jceps.com/index.php?pageID=home

National Education Association (NEA)
America's oldest and largest organization committed to advancing public education. NEA has 2.3 million members who teach at every level of education, from preschool to university — www.nea.org/index.html

Standardized testing

NCLB reform proponents also assert that standardized testing provides both a 'quality indicator' to the consumer and 'objective assessments' of student learning within education markets. In *No Child Left Behind: A Parents' Guide* (U.S. Department of Education, 2003a), parents are told that standardized tests are a valid and reliable means of assessing students' learning, superior to teacher-generated assessments. *The Guide* advises parents that NCLB 'will give them objective data' through standardized testing (ibid.: 12). Further, objective data from tests are necessary because 'many parents have children who are getting straight As, but find out too late that their child is not prepared for college. That's just one reason why NCLB gives parents objective data about how their children are doing' (ibid.: 12). Teachers, NCLB strongly implies, have not rigorously enforced standards nor accurately assessed students, therefore covering up their own and their students' failures. Moreover, test scores are useful to parents because 'parents will know how well learning is occurring in their child's class. They will know information on how their child is progressing compared to other children' (ibid.: 9). Because teachers, NCLB claims, have relied too often on their own assessments, standardized test scores will also benefit them. NCLB 'provides teachers with independent information about each child's strengths and weaknesses. With this knowledge, teachers can craft lessons to make sure each student meets or exceeds standards' (ibid.: 9).

Assessing teachers and students

Standardized testing is promoted as a means of assessing the quality of students, teachers and schools, thus ensuring that all children are treated fairly. Such a sentiment is reflected in Bush's recent statement that NCLB prevents 'children from being shuffled through our schools without understanding whether or not they can read and write and add and subtract ... That's unfair to the children' (U.S. Department of Education, 2006a: 3).

As standardized testing ostensibly provides educators with objective information about students' learning (the test results are rarely provided in the same academic year) and enables families to choose schools that are successfully educating children, NCLB's reforms are touted as improving educational opportunities for all students and closing the achievement gap between white students and students of colour. Paige, who as an African-American lends credibility to these claims, argued that NCLB improves education for all children, especially African-Americans.

> We have an educational emergency in the United States of America. Nationally, blacks score lower on reading and math tests than their white peers. But it doesn't have to be that way. We need to collectively focus our attention on the problem....We have to make sure that every single child gets our best attention. We also need to help African-American parents understand how this historic new education law can specifically help them and their children. (U.S. Department of Education, 2003b)

But, whether NCLB and similar reforms emphasizing high-stakes exams and accountability were actually designed to increase fairness and equality can be questioned. First, both neo-liberal and neo-conservative organizations have stated that their real goal is to use testing and accountability to portray public schools as failing and to push for privatizing education provided through competitive markets. Second, evidence suggests that our educational system is becoming more, not less, unequal with a higher drop-out rate for students of colour and students living in poverty, who are also more likely to be subjected to curricula and pedagogical practices that are less demanding, such as *Success for All* and *America's Choice*.

The undermining of public education and promoting markets and privatization

For many neo-liberals the ultimate goal of the recent reforms is to convert the educational system into markets and, as much as possible, privatize educational services (Johnson and Salle, 2004). In the US, both neo-conservative and neo-liberal organizations have attacked public schools and teachers with the goal of replacing public education with private education. For many of them, vouchers (funds provided parents to use towards tuition for private schools) and charter schools (publicly funded privately administered schools) are the first step towards privatizing schools. For example, Milton Friedman, in *Public Schools: Make Them Private* (1995), advocated vouchers as a way 'to transition from a government to a market system'. Freidman states:

> Our elementary and secondary education system needs to be totally restructured. Such a reconstruction can be achieved only by privatizing a major segment of the educational system – i.e. by enabling a private, for-profit industry to develop that will provide a wide variety of learning opportunities and offer effective competition to public schools. (cited in Johnson and Salle, 2004: 8)

Others call for the immediate elimination of public education. Richard Eberling (2000), president of the Foundation for Economic Education, in *It's Time to Put Public Education Behind Us*, writes:

> It's time, therefore, to rethink the entire idea of public schooling in America. It's time to consider whether it would be better to completely privatize the entire educational process from kindergarten through to Ph.D ... The tax dollars left in the hands of the citizenry would then be available for families to use directly to pay for their child's education. The free market would supply an infinitely diverse range of educational vehicles for everyone. (cited in Johnson and Salle, 2004: 8)

Some privatization advocates specifically anticipate that the high number of schools designated as failing to make AYP will lead to calls for privatizing schools. Howard Fuller, founder of the pro-voucher organization Black Alliance for Educational Options (BAEO), in a 2002 interview with the National Governors Association, said: 'Hopefully, in years to come the [NCLB] law will be amended to allow families to choose private schools as well as public schools' (cited in Miner, 2004: 11).

Privatization

Privatization also plays a role in other aspects of NCLB. Schools failing to achieve AYP lose federal funding for tutors. Instead, tutoring is provided by for-profit and non-profit community organizations, some of which have religious affiliations. The U.S. Department of Education earmarked 2.5 billion dollars for private sector tutoring in 2005–6. But one analysis concludes that many corporations did not have a 'viable business plan' and that there is great difficulty in providing private tutoring services (Borja, 2006: 5). Furthermore, schools face the prospect of having their administrations taken over by outside private for-profit organizations, such as the Edison Corporation.

Leaving children behind

As NCLB comes up for reauthorization, supporters assert that it is achieving its goal of improving student learning and closing the achievement gap. However, as I will too briefly argue in this section, the evidence suggests otherwise. The achievement gap between the US and other countries is not narrowing, but widening; school curricula are becoming narrower; and the achievement gap between white students and students of colour is not narrowing as quickly as it was pre-NCLB. In fact, on some measures the gaps are actually widening. Moreover, by blaming education for the outsourcing of jobs to other countries and the demise of decent paying jobs and the loss of healthcare diverts attention from efforts to solve America's economic and social problems.

Narrowing of the curriculum

Since many schools, but particularly urban schools, must focus on raising test scores in order to avoid sanctions, and other similarly high-scoring schools are drawn into a competitive market, it remains true that in most schools aspects of curriculum and pedagogy have been narrowed and simplified as teachers teach towards the test. Subjects that are either not tested under NCLB, such as art, music, social studies and history, are often given little or no attention. In literacy, elementary schools that receive Federal funding are limited to using the curricula approved by the Bush administration's Department of Education. These are scripted curricula that undermine teachers' skills and knowledge and their ability to respond to differences in students' culture and abilities. These pedagogical reforms have resulted, not surprisingly, in a decline in student learning and achievement as compared to before NCLB.

While NCLB proponents argued that the reforms would close the educational achievement gap between the US and other countries, the emphasis on teaching to tests that emphasize recall and factual content seems to have negatively impacted students' abilities to problem solve. On the Program in International Student Assessment (PISA), assessments designed to evaluate students' ability to apply knowledge to new problems, the US has fallen further behind other counties. The US now ranks 21st of 30 OECD countries in science and 25th of 30 in mathematics (Baldi et al., 2007).

A second indicator that the gap between the US and other countries is widening is the astonishing decline from having the highest university participation in the world to 14th, a decline that can be attributed to other countries expanding their post-secondary education systems and providing it to students at a lower cost. While 60 per cent of US high school graduates go off to university, only 30 per cent gain a baccalaureate degree, significantly fewer than the 50 per cent who earn degrees in OECD countries (Douglass, 2006). Similarly, over the past several decades the percentage of an age cohort graduating from US high schools has essentially remained the same while most OECD countries have had substantial increases passing the US (OECD, 2007). In some states, the percentage of students graduating from high school has decreased. In New York, for example, the graduation rate hovers just above 50 per cent (Haney, 2003).

Standards

NCLB supporters also asserted that it would improve overall student learning and close the achievement gap between white students and students of colour. Again, data suggest that neither of these outcomes have occurred. On the National Assessment of Educational Progress (NAEP), a nation-wide test given to samples of students, the annual rate of gain on the fourth and eighth-grade reading and mathematics achievement tests have decreased significantly from the pre-NCLB years (1999–2002) to the post-NCLB years (2002–7). Gains in mathematics scores have declined and gains on the eighth-grade exam on reading tests have stalled (Smith, 2007). Increases in students' scores have either ended or are increasing at a slower rate than pre-NCLB.

Moreover, given the Bush administration's stated goal of closing the achievement gap, the university enrolment rates by race and ethnicity reveal that while white, black and Hispanics in the late 1970s enrolled in university at almost equal rates, the enrolment gap has increased since then, and particularly in the most recent years for which we have data. The current gap is nearing 20 per cent (Forum for Education and Democracy, 2008: 4).

Claims of success

However, none of these data prevents the Bush administration and the Department of Education from claiming that NCLB is a success. In April 2006, the current Secretary of

Education, Margaret Spellings stated: 'This law is helping us learn what works in our schools. And clearly, high standards and accountability are working. Over the last five years, our 9-year-olds have made more progress in reading than in the previous 28 combined' (U.S. Department of Education, 2006b). Spellings cites the same NAEP scores that I cite above which do indeed show a 7 per cent gain from the period of 1999–2004 to support her claim. In response, critics such as Bracey (2006) point out that no NAEP data was gathered in the first two years of NCLB and that NCLB was in effect for little more than a year before the 2004 testing, hardly enough time to take credit for all of the increase in the reading test scores for 9-year-olds in that time span. Further, if the 2004 scores are compared to 1980, the increase is only 4 per cent. Spellings also chose to compare the 2004 test scores to a previous low point (1999). Furthermore, she only refers to the gains in 9-year-old-test scores, omitting that in the same period there was no gain for 12-year-olds and a decline of three points for 17-year-olds (ibid.: 151–2).

Other studies contradict Spellings' claim. The Harvard Civil Rights Project (Lee, 2006) examined reading and mathematics results by race on the NAEP before and after the implementation of NCLB to reveal that NCLB failed to deliver on its promise of closing the achievement gap. In the foreword to the study, Orfield summarizes the study as concluding that under NCLB:

> neither a significant rise in achievement, nor closure of the racial achievement gaps is being achieved. Small early gains in math have reverted to the preexisting pattern. If that is true, all the pressure and sanctions have, so far, been in vain or even counterproductive.... On the issue of closing the gap for minority and poor children, a central goal of NCLB, there are also no significant changes since NCLB was enacted. (2006: 5–6)

Furthermore, NCLB serves neo-liberal goals of reducing the size of government by reducing public funding for education and social services by blaming past education policies for the loss of jobs to China and India. Rather than examining trade and economic policies, the Bush administration blames our schools for not educating our children as well as those in China and India. This shell game has damaged the welfare of children and families during the Bush administration.

> How does the American administration's justification for NCLB compare to the British government's justification for its policies?
> What are the similarities and differences?

Over the last decade regional and federal policies have failed to provide access to living-wage jobs, decent housing and health care (Anyon, 2005; Hursh, 2006). In the US our cities are economically, racially and spatially segregated with people of colour geographically separated from well-paying jobs and lacking public transportation to get to them (Lipman, 2003). Consequently, whole urban populations face restricted possibilities with underfunded schools and low-paying jobs. In the US, almost half the people who earn poverty zone wages work full-time and year-round (Anyon, 2005: 19). People are poor not because they do not make an effort, but because there are few jobs that pay a living wage. Consequently, children are increasingly likely to be homeless, going hungry and without healthcare. During that time, the percentage of homeless people has increased by 87 per cent, the percentage showing up at food pantries increased by 76 per cent, and people without healthcare 12 per cent. Nearly one-fourth of US children live in families below the poverty line, more than in any other industrialized country. Moreover, class disparity increased to the highest level since the Census Bureau began publishing such data in 1967 and disparity based on race and gender increased. 'One was 158 per cent more likely to be in poverty if Black, Hispanic or Asian' (Wollman et al., 2007). However, the Bush response to economic and social problems has been to privatize services, as he did in New Orleans after Hurricane Katrina.

Alternatives

Instead of educational reforms, like NCLB, that focus on high-stakes standardized testing and privatizing schools and educational administration, and reducing social services and ignoring the real structural and economic conditions that exacerbate inequality and undermine efforts to provide for one's family, we can undertake reforms based on what we know works educationally and socially (Hursh, 2005, 2006).

How not to leave children behind

The tragedy of NCLB is not only the harm that it has caused to teachers, students, families and schools over the past six years, but the opportunities lost to build on the reforms that have demonstrated real improvements in student learning. As I have argued elsewhere (Hursh, 2008), NCLB and similar reforms emphasizing high-stakes standardized testing have been imposed at a time when many of John Dewey's ideas regarding the school as a community, interdisciplinary learning and authentic assessment were not only being successfully implemented in public schools (such as the Urban Academy in New York City), the schools that make up the Performance Assessment Consortium and the schools described in Mike Rose's *Possible Lives: The Promise of Public Education in America* (1995), but also at a time when research has been validating these innovative, interdisciplinary teaching approaches. For example, the National Research Council's commissioned reports on teaching, learning and assessment conclude that we now understand 'the nature of competent performance and the principles of knowledge organization that underlie people's abilities to solve problems in a wide variety of areas', and how best to teach and assess students' learning (2001: 4). Its report, *Knowing What Students Know: The Science and Design of Educational Assessment*, specifically recommends against over relying on standardized exams to assess students:

> Policy makers are urged to recognize the limitations of current assessment, and to support the development of new systems of multiple assessments that would improve their ability to make decisions about education programs and the allocation of resources. Important decisions about individuals should not be based on a single test score. Policy makers should invest instead in the development of assessment systems that use multiple measures of student performance, particularly when high stakes are attached to the results. (2001: 310)

Schools that make up the Performance Assessment Consortium emphasize evaluating students by examining student work and developing a wide range of academic goals that extend beyond the basic subjects to include citizenship and community service. Furthermore, teachers often team-teach with other teachers in class periods that are typically twice as long as the traditional 45-minute period in secondary schools. Lastly, the schools tend to be about one-fifth the size of traditional schools, allow the teachers and students to create a community in which they come to know one another as teachers and learners.

The damage caused by NCLB

Furthermore, teachers and parents increasingly recognize that NCLB causes more harm than good. In the annual *Phi Delta Kappan* Poll (Rose and Gallup, 2007) on the public's attitudes towards the public schools conducted in June 2007, 40 per cent of those polled have a 'somewhat or very unfavourable' opinion of NCLB while 31 per cent had a 'somewhat or very favourable' opinion. Also, the more familiar respondents were with NCLB, the more negative their view. Given that those with an unfavourable opinion had increased from 31 to 40 per cent over the previous year, it may well be the case that over 50 per cent of people now hold an unfavourable view. Consequently, even though NCLB was up for reauthorization this autumn, the Republican president and Democratic congress were not able to act on it and NCLB continues, temporarily, as is. However, the new president and congress, beginning in spring 2009, will need either to reform the act or scrap it all together.

Forum for Education and Democracy

The Forum for Education and Democracy is just one of the groups offering proposals for how federal education policy should change under the new administration. *The Forum* is an education think-tank composed of professors and former teachers dedicated to renewing

American's commitment to strong public schools and they recently released their report *Democracy at Risk: The Need for a New Federal Policy in Education* (2008). The report reveals the harms caused by the last quarter century of education policies, but particularly since NCLB.

In response, they argue that the federal government should focus on ensuring equal educational opportunity and building knowledge for good practice:

This federal support should occur through:

1. Investments and incentives for more equitable access to high-quality schools.
2. A set of intensive initiatives to develop a world-class education workforce.
3. A forward-looking agenda for educational research, innovation, and dissemination.
4. New strategies that enable communities to engage with and be accountable to their local schools.

In the report, they outline specific proposals for teacher preparation and continuing professional development, reorganizing schools to build on teachers' expertise, multiple assessments, equalizing school spending, for improving post-secondary education and educational research. They also argue that investing in education is necessary if we are to counter the increasing number of students who are dropping out of secondary schools and ending up unemployed or adding to the largest prison population in the world. Currently, one in one hundred Americans are incarcerated and 'several states are now spending as much on corrections as they do on higher education and the nation is spending about $44 billion annually on corrections' (Forum for Education and Democracy, 2008: 9). Correction costs increased over 900 per cent between 1980 and 2000 (ibid.: ix).

Activity

Compare and contrast the approaches taken in the NCLB initiative with the approaches taken by the UK government in relation to academic underachievement – (of different socio-economic and ethnic groups) through such programmes as the Academies initiative and other significant curriculum projects.

1. What similarities can you identify?
2. Can you identify the underlying ideologies?

What is needed, then, are educational, economic and social policies that restore the government's central role in providing the structural and human conditions for developing strong schools, healthy families and productive workers. To do otherwise will only continue to leave children behind.

Key Points

- NCLB is the largest federal education initiative in the history of the US
- NCLB affects nearly every aspect of elementary and secondary education
- A central feature of NCLB is formal testing that is now required of schools
- The test scores are detailed and grouped in a variety of ways, for example, gender and ethnicity
- The test scores are used to identify if a school has made AYP
- There is a strong correlation between the test scores and the social-economic status of the children taking the test
- The schools that are identified as failing as a result of the AYP figures are almost always in poor urban districts
- The consequences for failure on two consecutive years is school closure and the transfer of the children to another school
- NCLB is touted as the US Government's response to increased global competition
- Test scores are identified as being equivalent to educational standards
- The justification for NCLB – overcoming poor levels of educational attainment of the poor and ethnic minority groups, has not occurred
- NCLB is in effect a mechanism to privatize the state school system
- Evidence also suggests that NCLB is actually doing more harm than good, educationally speaking
- Alternative educational policies would address the needs of communities through investment in education and the government taking a leading role.

Further Reading

Hursh, D. (2008) *High-Stakes Testing and the Decline of Teaching and Learning: The Real Crisis in Education*, Lanham, MD: Rowman and Littlefield.

Peter Sacks (2007) *Tearing Down the Gates: Confronting the Class Divide in American Education*, Berkeley: University of California Press.

Kenneth Saltman (2005) *Edison Schools*, London: Routledge.

Paul Street (2005) *Segregated Schools*, London: Routledge.

References

Anyon, J. (2005) *Radical Possibilities: Public Policy, Urban Education and a New Social Movement*, New York: Routledge.

Baldi, S., Yin, J., Skerner, M., Green, P. and Herget, D. (2007) *Highlights from PISA 2006: Performance of U.S. 15-year-old Students in Science, Mathematics, Literacy in an International Context*, Washington, DC: National Center for Educational Statistics, Institute of Education Sciences, U.S. Department of Education.

Borja, R. (2006, December 20) 'Market for NCLB tutoring falls short of expectations', *Education Week*, 26 (16): 5 and 13.

Bracey, G. (2006, October) 'The 16th Bracey report on the condition of public education', *Phi Delta Kappan*, 151–66.

Center for Community Change (2006, September), *Dismantling a Community*, Washington, DC: Center for Community Change. Available at: www.communitychange.org

Douglass, J. A. (2006) *The Waning of America's Higher Education Advantage, Paper CSHE-9-06*, Berkeley: Center for Studies in Higher Education, University of California.

Eberling, R. M. (2000) 'It's time to put public education behind us', *Future of Freedom Foundation Commentaries*. Available at: www.fff.org/comment/ed0200f.asp

Education Review (2003, September 26) *International Report, U.S. Office of Education Listserve*. Available at: http://ed.gov.nclb (accessed 3 Oct. 2003).

The Forum for Education and Democracy (2008, April) *Democracy at Risk: The Need for a New Federal Policy in Education*, retrieved from www.forumforeducation.org/resources/index.php?item=427&page=32

Friedman, M. (1995, June 23) 'Public schools: make them private', *Cato Briefing paper* no. 23. Available at: www.cato.org/pubs/briefs/bp-023.html

Haney, W. (2003, September 23) 'Attrition of students from New York Schools. Invited testimony at public hearing, New York Senate, Standing Committee on Education', *Regents Learning Standards and High School Graduation Requirements*. Available at: www.timeoutfromtesting.org/testimonies/923_Testimony_Haney.pdf (accessed 5 Oct. 2003).

Hursh, D. (2005) 'The growth of high-stakes testing, accountability and education markets and the decline of educational equality', *British Educational Research Journal*, 31 (5): 605–22.

Hursh, D. (2006) 'The crisis in urban education: resisting neoliberal policies and forging democratic possibilities', *Educational Researcher*, 35 (4): 19–25.

Hursh, D. (2007a) 'Assessing the impact of No Child Left Behind and other neoliberal reforms in education', *American Educational Research Journal*, 44 (3): 493–518.

Hursh, D. (2007b) 'Exacerbating inequality: the failed promise of the No Child Left Behind Act', *Race, Ethnicity and Education*, 10 (3): 295–308.

Hursh, D. (2008) *High-Stakes Testing and the Decline of Teaching and Learning: The Real Crisis in Education*, Lanham, MD: Rowman and Littlefield.

Johnson, D. C. and Salle, L. M. (2004) *Responding to the Attack on Public Education and Teacher Unions: A Commonweal Institute Report* (Menlo Park, CA: Commonweal Institute). Available at: www.commonwealinstitute.org/IssuesEducation.htm

Lee, J. (2006) 'Tracking achievement gaps and assessing the impact of NCLB on the gaps: An in-depth look into national and state reading and math outcome trends', Boston, MA: The Civil Rights Project of Harvard University.

Lipman, P. (2003) *High Stakes Education: Inequality, Globalization, and Urban School Reform*, New York: Routledge.

Miner, B. (2004) 'Seed money for conservatives', *Rethinking Schools*, 18 (4): 9–11.

National Research Council (2001) 'Knowing what students know: the science and design of educational assessment', in J. W. Pelligrino, N. Chudowsky and R. Glaser (eds), *Committee on the Foundations of Assessment*, Washington, DC: National Academy Press.

Organisation for Economic Cooperation and Development (2007) *Education at a Glance*, Paris: OECD.

Orfield, G. (2006) *Forward, Tracking Achievement Gaps and Assessing the Impact of NCLB on the Gaps: An In-Depth Look into National and State Reading and Math Outcome Trends*, Boston, MA: Civil Rights Project of Harvard University.

Rose, L. C. and Gallup, A. M. (2007) 'The 39th annual Phi Delta Kappa/Gallup poll of the public's attitudes toward the public schools', *Phi Delta Kappan*, 89 (1): 33–45.

Rose, M. (1995) *Possible Lives: The Promise of Public Education in America*, Boston: Houghton Mifflin.

Smith, M. (2007) *What about NCLB?*, Palo Alto, CA: Hewlett Foundation.

U.S. Department of Education, Office of the Secretary (2003a) *NCLB: Parents Guide to NCLB: What to Know and Where to Go*, Washington, DC.

U.S. Education Department, press release (2003b) *ABC Radio Network Launch Education Campaign to Help Close Achievement Gap*. Retrieved from www.ed.gov/PressReleases/08-2003/08262003.html (accessed 29 Aug. 2003).

U.S. Department of Education, Office of the Press Secretary (2006a) *President Bush Discusses No Child Left Behind*, Washington, DC. Available at: www.ed.gov/news/releases/2006/10/20061005-6.html

U.S. Department of Education (2006b) Remarks by Secretary Spellings at No Child Left Behind Summit. Available at: www.ed.gov.new. Search on 'press releases'.

Wollman, N., Yoder, B. and Brumbaugh-Smith, J. (2007) *The 2007 National Index of Violence and Harm*, North Manchester, IN: Manchester College.

Index